DISILLUSIONED INDIA

DHAN GOPAL MUKERJI has also written

VISIT INDIA WITH ME
MY BROTHER'S FACE
CASTE AND OUTCAST
THE FACE OF SILENCE
A SON OF MOTHER INDIA ANSWERS
SECRET LISTENERS OF THE EAST
DEVOTIONAL PASSAGES FROM THE
    HINDU BIBLE

For Children

GAY NECK *Awarded the Newberry Medal, 1927.*
    (Illustrated by Boris Artzybasheff. Selected as
    one of the best illustrated books of 1927 by the
    American Institute of Graphic Arts.)

GHOND THE HUNTER
    (Illustrated by Boris Artzybasheff. Selected as
    one of the best illustrated books of 1928 by the
    American Institute of Graphic Arts.)

KARI, THE ELEPHANT
JUNGLE BEASTS AND MEN
HARI, THE JUNGLE LAD
HINDU FABLES
THE CHIEF OF THE HERD

Published by E. P. DUTTON & Co., INC.

DISILLUSIONED
INDIA

BY

DHAN GOPAL MUKERJI

Author of "Visit India With Me," "My Brother's Face,"
"A Son of Mother India Answers," etc.

NEW YORK
E. P. DUTTON & CO., INC.

FIRST EDITION

DEDICATED
TO
KAMALA NEHRU

CONTENTS

LETTER   PAGE

I. WHY I REVISITED INDIA 15

II. A HINDU SHOW 35

III. A NATIONALIST CONFERENCE . . . 45

IV. DISENCHANTED EYES 53

V. BAZARS 61

VI. JAWAHARLAL NEHRU OF ALLAHABAD . . 71

VII. POLITICAL DISILLUSION 79

VIII. WHAT THE OFFICIAL BRITISH MIND BE-
LIEVES 93

IX. KUMBHA-MELA, A LEGACY OF OUR RE-
LIGIOUS PAST 101

X. THE TWO NEHRUS 109

XI. A BRITISH POINT OF VIEW 117

XII. OUR MODERATE AND LIBERAL POINT OF
VIEW 125

XIII. A DANCER 133

XIV. VISIT TO THE VILLAGERS OF THE UNITED
PROVINCES 139

XV. BENARES 147

XVI. A HOLY MAN 153

XVII. INTRANSIGENT PEASANTS 159

8   CONTENTS

LETTER   PAGE
XVIII. BREAKERS OF THE SALT LAW 173
 XIX. AS A BEGGAR SEES IT   183
  XX. AS A HOLY MAN SEES IT   .   .   . 193
 XXI. THINGS THAT MATTER 207

     CONCLUSION!   219

     AS A PRINCE SEES IT   223

FOREWORD

INDIA today affords a most interesting example of the effect of the contact of Western civilization on an Eastern culture after two centuries. Today as a result of English influence many young Indians desire to achieve for India the ideals for which England has stood: liberty expressed through self-government, abolition of caste, scientific living, and emancipation of women. The Eastern youth has been taught that much of the freedom both in Europe and America has been won through violent warfare. And as a consequence, there is a continual tendency on the part of our youth to break out in armed resistance regardless of whether warfare will result in victory or not. The Indian youth is of an heroic strain and quite ready to die for his country. The stories of such heroes as George Washington and Oliver Cromwell have kindled his enthusiasm. In following these heroes he tends to follow the methods of violence adopted by them.

In this struggle of violence which has arisen, Gandhi stands as an exponent of the ancient ideals of the East. To him the spiritual and the aesthetic future of India is far more important than her material well-being. Gandhi has become convinced that the revolutionary

9

movement in India has grown so widespread that it
cannot be thwarted. And he therefore accepts it as
a fact, at the same time seeking to compel it to express
itself only through peaceful means. He has continually urged that the revolution should be non-violent.
He is in sympathy with all the social aims of a revolution: such as, abolition of caste and freedom of
women.

The writer, as a result of his visit to India, is not
satisfied that in case India is given virtual independence it can govern itself as well as Great Britain or
the United States is governed. But he feels convinced
that the teaching of liberty has gone so far that there
can be no question that dominion status ought to be
granted as a practical matter. The doctrines of Western
civilization have penetrated India so far that if virtual
independence is not granted, India will slip into revolutionary chaos. The situation is now developing there
as it did in the United States in the Eighteenth Century where the revolution was started without any
thought of separation from Great Britain. If in the
beginning of 1775 Britain had given the colonies a
status like that of Canada today, it is probable that
no revolution would have been fought and the United
States might very well be at the present time part of
the British Empire.

It is probable that the gravity of the present situation in India is not apprehended and appraised by the
British people in England in much the same manner

that it was not apprehended by the contemporaries of Lord North when they were faced with the intransigence of the thirteen colonies.

If the recent statements of the Viceroy, Lord Irwin, about considering proposals other than the recommendations of the Simon Commission had been made a year ago, they might well have satisfied all India. The Labor Party in Power in Britain at present still hopes that a solution can be worked out through peaceful negotiations, at the Round Table Conference, October, 1930. . . . In the meantime revolution supported by idealists who are ready to sacrifice all for their country is an ever-augmenting danger.

LETTER I

WHY I REVISITED INDIA

LETTER I

WHY I REVISITED INDIA

WHEN the Indian National Congress under the leadership of Pandit Jawaharlal Nehru—who happens to be a friend of mine—declared independence at the end of 1929, it became imperative for me to make a pilgrimage to my native land.

Hitherto I had visualized India as a dominion, like Canada, within the British Empire. Now that a large section of my countrymen had decided to work for a purpose greater than Dominion Status it behooved me to study their psychology in order to make a report of it to that section of the American public who read my books. I had also another purpose to accomplish: I wanted to see a person of great spiritual significance, that is, my Guru. It has been the firm intention of my soul to receive his blessings and no doubt this consideration weighed more heavily with me than any other.

Before sailing from New York I communicated with an American friend of mine, Mr. John Earl, who is a Pali scholar and an artist. It was my good fortune that he could start East at a very short notice. Since he had been to India and Ceylon several times before, the bother of seeing the sights we could easily abandon.

This simplified our plan and brought it within the limits of my physical strength. For a man who had been a partial invalid for nearly two years hates the very thought of long journeys to ruins and romantic spots. He who has the slightest touch of ill-health looks at historic scenes and works of art through a veil of irritability. "Even the Taj Mahal fails to soothe the savage twinges of rheumatism," says a humorist.

Bearing this in mind Mr. Earl and I set out of Venice for India. In order to introduce my friend to the reader I should give a description of him. He is a gray-haired American of the most unbusinesslike appearance. Though belonging to no particular religious sect, he has kept up a steady habit of meditation two hours a day for over twenty-five years. His sculpture, specifically his Buddha that he has carved, is well known on the continent of Europe and in Ceylon. There is one Buddha of his which when shown to the world will compel universal praise.

The reason for his going to India at this time lay in his desire to see my India: our own religious order, and our daily spiritual activity in the monastery at Benares, a place where, though a Westerner, a friend of mine would not be forbidden to enter. Mr. Earl was as eager as myself to see the holy man who has been in silence for the past six years.

Having explained the feeling that drove me towards India, I shall quote from letters written to my family during my absence from America. The following pages do not constitute a work of art. They are notes on the present situation in India. They were written, if not in the most informal manner, at least very rapidly. I beg the reader to overlook their numerous blemishes. If he wishes to know what has led India to her present psychological state, he should consult "My Brother's Face," and "Visit India With Me." In chapter twelve of the former and in some chapters of the latter appeared certain predictions of mine which recent events have fulfilled.

On our arrival in Bombay a procession of Bombay Nationalist Youths received me with cries of "Gandhiki Jai!"—Victory to Gandhi. They waved their red-white-green flags mounted with three stars and a crescent. "What do they symbolize?" Mr. Earl asked me. In the midst of renewed shouts of "Victory to Gandhi!" I spoke very loudly to him, "White for Hindus, red or fire for the Zoroastrians, green and the crescent for the Mohammedans; and the three stars stand for Buddhism, Sikhism, and Christianity."

Just then I was startled by a strange biscuit-colored face of an Englishman watching me from behind. He had not been seen on our ship the two long weeks of our journey from Venice. He must have come on deck with the pilot.

That he belonged to the C. I. D., the British Indian Secret Police, was borne out by his behavior. No matter where I went, he followed me faithfully. From eight in the morning till past noon he accompanied me. I shall never forget his face. It was so nondescript that it seemed unique. The sun of India had turned his complexion yellow. The pupils of his eyes glinted with a topaz light. I was pursued nearly half a day by those eyes.

At last we landed. Then two English policemen in uniform, aided by an Indian detective, took charge of our bags, searching for seditious matter. In the meantime the arms of the nationalist youths engulfed me in their embrace. "Is it possible?" I asked myself again and again. "Is it possible that in India there are so many youths who are shedding their fears of the British and coming out openly for freedom? Am I hearing aright their cry, 'Long live complete independence—Puran Swaraja!' ?"

Since the ridiculous is only an inch behind the sublime, all my happiness was put to flight when the four C. I. D. officers began desecrating the contents of my baggage. Letters of my wife, child, and brother were read by each member of the Police as if they were newspapers. Clothes were searched for unearthing small firearms. In time, the humor of the situation dawned upon my mind. "Here," I spoke to my fellow-traveler, "is the real comedy of terrors." Earl answered, "My bag has some of my letters of introduction to Gandhi." I tried to frighten him. "They will not let you enter India if they find those letters." Earl: "That will be fun. I shall make our State Department resound with my shrieks of protest."

Here one of the English detectives shook a silver thing under my nose, demanding, "What's in this?"

"That," I said, "is my American whiskey flask."
Everybody present burst out laughing. I explained further: "It has no whiskey in it." It is strange how the
18th Amendment has made any mention of liquor a
source of jokes.

I am glad that I carried that flask with me. It estab-
lished the fact that I was "a regular fellow." Finding
me very simple, and harmless, the Police gave up
searching my baggage with great care. Apparently he
who carries an empty liquor bottle cannot be a revolutionary.

All the same, nearly two more hours were consumed
in going through Mr. Earl's baggage—I requested the
volunteers to furl their flags and go home. Seeing
that the examination of my friend's letters might go
on forever, they agreed with me and marched to their
headquarters away from the scorching heat of the
Custom House.

Now left alone with the police, a sense of desola-
tion seized me. "What a country!" I kept on repeating to myself, while letter after letter, taken out of
Mr. Earl's possession, was handed from one reader to
another. Of course the Pali words here and there
puzzled them so that they had to ask my friend about
their meaning. Every now and then he explained:
"That is Dukha, sorrow; the other is Sukkha, happiness. . . . What is this? It means Buddha."

I was getting very tired. A man who had been ailing
for months cannot stand in the noonday heat of India

for nearly four hours and be stared at in the bargain by Secret Service men, without feeling it.

But Dukha, sorrow, too, is brief. As if a divine apparition had descended upon us from nowhere, a sumptuously robed South Indian lady, strode towards us. Her green Sari, blue-black hair, and black eyes wrought enchantment before us. Though I had half-suspected her identity, I dared not speak. Then, as white water sings through black rocks, my ears were pierced by the words of my friend's wife.

"Indeed the gods are good, now that they have brought you to us. My lord commanded me to spread comfort before your feet. May I never fail to make your stay here most felicitous."

I saluted her, I hope with equal grace. But just then the porters were clamouring for their fee. They wanted two whole dollars. I protested. But they insisted that India had changed. "The cost of existence augments day by day. O upholder of discrimination, pay us what we ask."

"Brothers," I shouted in well-chosen Hindustani, "I admit I am the upholder of intelligence. But don't you think five rupees is too much?"

"We assure you, O diadem of insight, it is only just," they chorused.

I asked impatiently, "Do you really take me for a donkey?"

"But who said donkey?" they clamoured.

"Here are your three rupees, which are abundance itself. Now go, if you please," I begged them.

"You're stingy. You come from rich America, then offer us three rupees! What insult!"

"Listen to me, O tongue of a gold-finch," I thrust at them, "you may take me for a donkey, but like a real donkey I did not leave my hind legs behind."

"You speak truth!" they exclaimed in unison. "Give us three rupees! Your tongue has beguiled us."

My friend's wife, Kalyana Delei, cast a glance of pity at their receding figures and scorn at me:

"Always bargaining?"

I sought to soothe her mind:

"I learnt it in the U. S. A. where I bargain with publishers and editors."

Mme. Delei said, "Come, Mr. Earl's inquisition is just over. It is long past midday. I shall take you to your hotel. Rest all afternoon. We have planned something pleasant for you to behold this evening."

But no rest was permitted us that afternoon. For the captain of the Bombay Youth League, Mr. Allimir, called on us with his colleagues. They were all young men below thirty, representing nearly all castes and every religion. Allimir himself was a Mohammedan. It pleased me immensely to see a Mohammedan Chief of Staff. He saluted me with the elegance of a noble-man of the Moghul period. His long homespun coat, peaked white cap, and sandaled feet, in fact every-thing about him was in keeping with his position of a captain. All the others, though not so magnificent in appearance, were dressed in khaki shirts and short trousers.

After the captain had taken his seat, the rest of his colleagues squatted on the floor with Mr. Earl and myself. Thus seated at the feet of the Commandant, we listened to what he had to say. But he was quite surprised to hear that I was too ill to go to see Gandhi.

"I know, I know," I protested. "But my nerves have gone to pieces. I am really ill. Can't sleep at night. I shall not present my letter to Gandhi. Nor shall I ask the Viceroy for an interview. I must save my waning strength to go to my holy man in Benares, and to Nehru, your President. Gandhi is on his march to the Salt Lick, near Dandi, far away from anywhere. Dandi sounds like a parody on Tipperary."

Allimir went on exhorting me all the same:

"Twelve hours' train ride, then half a day's march —all that is nothing when one thinks of calling on Buddha, Christ, Saint Francis, or Mohammed."

The captain was a most persuasive talker. Some of his colleagues now took a hand in persuading me to go. Said one of them:

"It is a new phenomenon, the present incarnation of Gandhi: it was unforeseen. He has converted about five million Gujratis into a compact army of nonviolence. The military may murder their children, rape their women; yet the men will neither run away nor will they commit violence."

"Are not the Gujratis his own people?" asked Mr. Earl.

"Yes," answered Allimir. "He comes from an old Gujrati family of Banias, traders. But Gandhi's immediate forbears were prime ministers, and councilors of the Gujrati kingdoms, Porbundar, Nirmukha, and Saptaraj. In a sense he too has renounced wealth and position like Buddha."

"But, O core of enthusiasm," I informed the gentlemen present, "I am here to see a holy man whom I have the premonition I am bound to find in Benares. I need the advice of a Guru for a very important step that I am contemplating. Him I hope to unearth in holy Kashi, Benares. Next in importance to him is Pandit Jawaharlal Nehru, the President of the Indian National Congress. I must save my slender strength for those two persons. Before I am worse I must get to Benares. And on my way thither I shall see Jawaharlal Nehru in Prayaga, Allahabad. Allahabad lies directly on my route. Please do not press me to visit anyone else."

All the same argued Allimir: "You will never see Gandhi, who is now marching as Buddha marched through India. Every town that he passes lifts its face to him like a lotus to the risen sun. I will never forget what I beheld last week. Can anyone imagine millions of men, women, and children stirred up by a lean man of sixty-two, homely, of short stature, all his front teeth gone, leaning on a tall staff, trampling through dusty roads? Well, that is Gandhi: Not pompous, not polysyllabic, just a pilgrim on his last journey. When you walk with him a light seems to emanate from him and fills you with its deep radiance."

In order to penetrate the meaning of his previous comparison of Gandhi with Buddha, I asked: "Why do you link the founder of Buddhism with Gandhi? Buddha as far as I know avoided the blunder of Plato: he never wasted his breath on any kind of politics, either of an ideal Republic or of a practical Tammany Hall."

The word Tammany put the fat in the fire. Allimir blazed forth like a volcano.

"You are pleased to be humorous. My dear Sir, Smith or Coolidge are as far from Gandhi as Machiavelli is from Saint Francis."

In order to make my meaning clear, I said to Allimir: "What is it you are trying to convey when you identify a cosmic symbol like Buddha with a human person like Gandhi?"

Now he understood. His eyes, gray-black, gleamed with pleasure. His lips, thin as razor blades, twitched with the foretaste of his own eloquence. Then he plunged into his subject.

"Buddha, through some alchemy of the Indian spirit set in the heart of the race the image of an ideal. This has not changed during twenty-five centuries that have passed since. The ideal Indian must be a man who has renounced all materialism. He may do so in a palace like the emperor Marcus Aurelius, or like Socrates, the philosopher. But the Indian spirit

demands that he should be free of all possessions and
of every vanity. That is why whenever we behold a
man swaying our masses profoundly, he is never a
king, nor a rich merchant. It is invariably a sanyasin
like Kabir, Nanak, Chaitanya, or Gandhi, a half-naked
man walking, leaning on a staff. In short, a beggar is
our ideal: Gandhi is the return of that omnipotent
image to our midst. That is why wherever he goes,
all distinctions of caste, creed, and sex vanish. Pariah
and Brahmin, Hindu and Moslem, women and men—
all unite to do him homage. Besides, all try to do
what he tells them. In the whole British Empire he
is more powerful than any Prince of Wales, any Viceroy, and any emperor. He is our ancient ideal come to
life. Buddha set it before India, when he renounced
his throne and kingdom and went in search of God.
For two thousand years and more, that has been our
conception of a leader. Asoka, emperor though he was,
sacrificed a whole empire for the sake of spreading
his religion through tolerance, love, and self-sacrifice.
Later, Emperor Akbar, true to the spirit of India,
sought to establish a religion as the basis of his empire.
Gandhi is Buddha, Asoka, and Akbar come again.
His secret lies in the fact that he is a beggar as was
Buddha. Our ideal today is what it has been for centuries."

As if he had made his peroration, Allimir rose to
take his leave. But I insisted that he should answer one
more question. This he did without sitting down:

"You want to know the truth? Well, this is the honest truth. As long as Gandhi is at liberty we shall work hard for a non-violent revolution. But the moment he is put in jail we shall act, each group, according to our own convictions."

"Why such a queer division of policies?" Mr. Earl wanted to know.

Allimir answered, still standing: "All of us pledged him that we would work for his kind of revolution as long as he or Nehru were in the lead. But once they are put in jail there will not be any person of their calibre to control the violent fellows. So the violent revolutionist will go his way; and we shall go ours. Each group will do what it thinks right. This is my honest belief. Farewell, farewell."

Slowly he strode out of the room, followed by his colleagues. After they had gone my friend and I looked out of the window. It was past the sunset hour. Across the bay hung Venus, the evening star, against a green sky. Below us, vendors were crying in tenor, "Citron for sale, colorless colour—Narangi—oranges for sale!" Above them rose the falsetto of the mendicant Mohammedan Saint "Maula Mooskeel Asan"—"May God remove all difficulties from our paths."

Soon after the night's blackness had blotted out the Indian Ocean from sight, we went down to meet Kalyana Delei at a meeting of *Pardanashins,* women in strict seclusion. It was a pleasure to drive through the streets of Bombay, listening to sounds. Above the drone and groan of many motor cars, like the wail of a mortally wounded wolf, rose the Muezzin's call to prayer. Shrieks of beaten bronze ran out of innumerable Hindu Temples. Thud of drums from nahabat Khana, gateways, the threne of stringed instruments, sarangis and harps, poured in streams from balconies and housetops. And riding those sounds as "the rains plain rivers" sped from lane to lane the falsetto cries of Pagaudiwallah, sweetmeat-vendors.

Alas, our study and enjoyment of sounds was made too brief by our arrival at the ladies' meeting. As we entered the hallway of the palatial mansion of Mr. Dhuni,[1] I warned Mr. Earl, "Poor men that we are, we shall be kept on one side of a screen while the ladies hold their meeting on the other. We sha'n't see a face. These are women behind the Purdah."

As I had predicted, so it turned out. We were ushered into a room full of men. After my friend and I had squatted on the floor, we looked around to locate the Purdah. Lo! there it was, a screen made of iridescent beads. Behind it I could surmise were seated, hidden from men's eyes, aristocratic Mohammedan, Marwari, Rajput, and other Northern women who strictly observe seclusion. Now as I listened intently to the talk of the men around us, I learned from them that the ladies were debating among themselves a very important matter.

[1] See "Visit India With Me," Chapters III, IV, V, for a fuller description of Dhuni.

A white-haired Rajput gentleman who sat near us said to his neighbor: "Let it happen. It was bound to come. It will shock us. But let it."

The gentleman who answered him was a young Mohammedan from the Punjab dressed in the costume of his province:

"It has come to Turkey, why not here? It was in Istamboul, Constantinople, that I witnessed it first. Khodaki Koodrat, as it pleases God."

But there was a Marwari, moneylender, who cackled about honour:

"Izzat is Izzat, honour is honour. Woman is the other name of honour. He who cheapens the most sacred thing will bring our race great harm."

"Nehi, Sahib," rejoined the Punjab. "No sir. In Turkey now they have a much finer sense of honour than before."

"What on earth are they talking about?" Mr. Earl demanded with eagerness.

"Something important is impending," I reassured him, I who was just as much in the dark as he. . .

The Marwari grumbled some more, "Our wives, mothers——"

Exactly in the manner of a theatrical performance, the curtain before us moved out of sight revealing in the blazing electric light over a hundred ladies in Mohammedan, Marwari, Rajput, and Punjab costumes. Almost all of them turned their heads as the men's glances fell on them. Now was the time to do

a tactful thing. In order to destroy the embarrassment
of the moment, impelled by a sudden inspiration, all
of us shouted: "Victory to Gandhi, Victory!"

After us cried all the women, "Mahatma Gandhiki
Jai, Mahatma Gandhiki Jai, Mahatma Gandhiki Jai!"
Three times.

Now that the assembled people were at their ease,
a young volunteer started a new cheer: "Down with
Purdah!" This cheer too was repeated three times.

Now the meeting began in right earnest. Kalyana
Delei rose from behind the assembled ladies and spoke
for ten minutes urging all present "to take a vow not
to observe women's seclusion any more" and "not to
wear anything made in England."

Both the vows were repeated in unison by the crowd
three times, for in order to make a statement binding
all Hindus repeat it thrice. Apparently the Indian
Mohammedans do not mind this superstition: They
too reiterated the vows as stated.

Now the enrollment of volunteers began. Some
dozen women had themselves enrolled then and there
for the task of picketing open saloons[2] and boycotting
shops that sold British goods. Seeing their wives enrolling, almost all the men had themselves enrolled on
the spot. It was a moving sight.

When the meeting was over, and most of the men
had taken their womenfolk home, there remained

---

[2] In India all the saloons are licensed by the government. It auctions
each license to the highest bidder.

/3276

some Marwari and Mohammedan women who wanted
me to speak on the "Women of America."

You remember, my old father's injunction, "Never
lay your tongue to the subject—woman." And I must
say that the greatest amount of froth that ever escapes
men's lips is generated by their discourse on womanhood. The Omniscient alone understands what woman
is; and we should leave it at that.

All the same I had to speak on the American
woman. This is what I said:

"In America two things struck me as worthy of our
imitation. They are the health of the children and the
vocational training of women. Every woman is trained
for another vocation besides marriage. And the thing
that all women see to is their children's food and
health. In India we need a revolution in hygiene
and infant dietetics. After they are a year old our children are exposed to the most unscientific food in the
world."

My speech was acclaimed by the women as if I was
the veriest oracle.

After having harangued them most earnestly, I
stopped, worn out. Earl had to take me home right
after it and put me to bed. No more public speaking
for me.

All the same that miserable speech of mine had
endeared me to many mothers. Result: I had to visit
many children's schools, and small meetings of women
the next few days. The interest in women's emanci-

pation has grown apparently under the stimulus of the Gandhi movement.

Remember,[3] I am not talking about South Indian women who have always had their liberty. It is of the women of North India who began secluding themselves after the Tartar invasion of the Thirteenth Century. Every meeting I went to was attended by the hitherto Purdanshin. It was inspiring to see them drop their veils.

Even if Gandhi is kept in prison the rest of his life this movement will go on. He has set moving such an urge for freedom among the women of Hindustan as has not been witnessed in our country for centuries. As this urge augments it will sweep all kinds of bondage, social and political, out of existence. The movement is not confined to any one class. When I went to the Parel factory women's meeting, I witnessed the same spectacle and greater enthusiasm there. The factory women are polyglot: Peshwari Mohammedans, Punjab Brahmins, Bengali Baboos—all asked me about the way the American woman runs her home and brings up children.

The awakening of proletariats is characterized by the same impatience in other large cities. Later on I found in Calcutta if not greater, at least an equal amount of unrest. Can you imagine Calcutta women, that is to say women of Bengal, who had observed strict Purdah for years, coming to a meeting of men

[3] See "Caste and Outcast."

to hear me talk on "The Women of America?" This happened. Then I was invited to talk to them exclusively at length regarding education and diet. All castes and all creeds were represented at this meeting. They sat unveiled before *Swiesh Boerji,* the poet, a few other men and myself. Then they questioned me for two hours. Just to tell you some more about the social progress that India is making, permit me to mention this stark fact. Among the members of the Labor Unions in Calcutta and Bombay you will find many women. They not only belong to the rank and file, but some of them are leaders. The President of the Scavengers' Union in Calcutta is a woman Ph.D.

A word about schools. The pity of it is that there are not enough of them. Though the hunger for education is intense, not more than twenty per cent of the children of school-going age of Bombay, our most progressive city, can be accommodated. Very few buildings are available. And even these are not any too healthy. I can show you places of learning that are fit for nothing save housing cattle. How people have the heart to send children there passes my understanding. But they will be replaced by better ones now that the women are coming out to fight for their rights. And fight they will. Every women's group, rich or poor, that I spoke to—oh, I had to speak no matter how I felt—was made up of no idlers. Most of them were earnest. The corners of their mouths and their jaws were set like those of the matrons of Rome.

LETTER II

A HINDU SHOW

LETTER II

A HINDU SHOW

OUR second night in Bombay we spent at a motion picture show to which Mme. Delei took us.

But before we reached there she drove us through some ancient lanes to give pleasure to our ears. We were driven slowly by the horse-dealers' stables whence rose many songs. A high-pitched voice sang some Hindustani words. We stopped our automobile in order to hear better, and saw a man busy at some work.

"What is he doing, O chauffeur?"

Our chauffeur answered us, "He is massaging his horse, and singing a few words."

Yes, the Sayce? The groom was repeating two short lines of a poem:

"Now the spider weaves the drapery where the emperor's
   mantle hung.
And the tower whence the haughty trumpet spoke is filled
   by the owl's hooting like an ill-tuned drum."

The song stopped as suddenly as it had begun. We drove on, slowly as before. And as I had anticipated, not far from our theatre near Baliwala's, we heard a street poet singing to a large audience of labourers these lines: "The long hair of night is not long enough

35

to hide my love. The white sword of day is not sharp enough to guard her from hurt. . . . This morsel of mischief, my heart, must be cut in two to shield her whom I love."

After this simple song of a common street singer how dared we enter a theatre? It was my patriotism that is to blame. I wanted to look at a hundred per cent Hindu film. And in these days of patriotism how could we patronize alien pictures?

The chief feature of the Deccan Playhouse this particular evening was the abundance of factory labourers of all creeds amongst its spectators. This being Saturday night they had come with their wives. It was immensely interesting. Even the Mohammedan workers had brought their wives who sat there "shameless," meaning with faces unveiled.

But what interested me most was the clatter of dialects. Hindustani, the common language of India, ran like a universal woof through Gujrati, Marathi, Posthu, and Urdoo. Each language had its key to which it was set. Posthu was always basso profundo, Gujrati always falsetto, Marathi was spoken in tenor, while Hindustani and Urdoo flitted from key to key as if they were at home everywhere in the mansion of music. The voices of the labourers rose several octaves it seemed; then went down again to silence. This happened more than once while we waited for the curtain to rise. It was during one of these spells of silence that some of the workers discovered Mme.

Delei. They started to greet her with shouts of "Victory." "Victory to Gandhi, Victory to Nehru, and Victory to India!" Hearing that a miniature riot was in the air the movie operator suddenly turned off the lights, and flashed on the screen a news reel. The mob was silent as suddenly as it had broken out into shouts a few minutes earlier.

The news reel told us of events all over the world. The Prince of Wales, the President of America, Henry Ford, and other well-known personages flashed in and out of our view. Suddenly there appeared a blank. A vivid white light vibrated in the dark theatre, followed by complete darkness. Soon the lights were turned on, apparently for some reason known only to itself. The mob set up a tremendous uproar. I thought they would bring the ceiling down on our heads.

"What are they yelling for?" I asked Kalyana Delei. She answered, "News reel of Gandhi's march."

Mr. Earl spoke his mind. "Where is it? I want to see it."

Mme. Delei: "Did you not see in the evening paper that the Censor has banned that particular reel? It will not be shown. The people are shouting in protest."

"No," groaned my friend, who was disappointed.

Now appeared on the stage a stocky man in Gandhi cap and white Khaddar, homespun, and started to make a speech.

He said, "O assembled civilized beings, we were

ordered by the police to suppress the news reel of Gandhi's March to Dandi. Since he is marching to break the Salt laws, the government considered a picture of him to be lawless. Therefore, O assembled civilized beings, this particular bit has been destroyed; which deprives you and me of seeing the march."

No sooner had he finished than the audience started cursing the proprietor of the theatre. "You are a half-brother to a mule, O grandfather of monkeys, O thou long snout, O eater of pigs, O incestuous ass!"

Fortunately the theatre was plunged into darkness again, and a long film was begun. It was entitled "The Sacrifice of Youth."

It was a most marvellous and the most sinister film. Though it rendered the episode, "Death of the Boy Abhimanyu," from the ancient Sanskrit epic Mahabharata, its style of rendering the written words into visual images was the subtlest propaganda for India's freedom by means of the sacrifice of the young manhood of the country. It was the most well-contrived piece of nationalist propaganda that I have seen. The fellow who made the film must have known his business. He knew how well-versed the Indian masses are in their ancient epics. They hear them recited everywhere almost every day. The movie director had taken advantage of that background of the people. Besides, he had given the British the impression that his film was about an episode of ancient India. Lo, the police censors had licensed its production! But anyone who knows both his Mahabharata and modern Gandhism can tell by looking at the picture that Abhimanyu, the boy-hero, was destroyed by the treachery of unscrupulous enemies.

There was another touch that was not to be overlooked—the boy-hero Abhimanyu's death is the crisis on which turns the final catastrophe of the Mahabharata in the same manner as the murder of Macduff's children in Shakespeare's *Macbeth*. All this had been weighed, calculated and exploited by the Indian filmproducer.

The sentiment that it roused in the audience was appalling. The psychic condition grew to be so full of resentment against the British that it almost became a living person before my eyes. Towards the end of the picture the audience began to shout, "The Hindu God and the Mohammedan God are one—Rama Rahim Ek Hai—Bharat Mataki Jai—Victory to India! Unite, Long live the Revolution."

Unable to bear the tension any longer, I led my friends out into the open, and there asked a taxi to drive us to the seashore.

Soon we left the car and began to walk up and down the beach. Ere I could feel under our feet the resignation of the sand, Kalyana Delei began to prophesy: "You can see that the nation will not remain non-violent if they put Gandhi and Jawaharlal Nehru, our president, into prison."

Her remark hurt me more than I can tell. I said,

"Friend, if you like to destroy the boys of India by starting the revolution, do so. But why do you destroy our women, second to none in the whole world?"

"What do you mean, Dhan Gopal?" queried my friend from America. "None of us was speaking of women."

"I am afraid I am confusing several ideas," I explained. "Today I was at a meeting of the lower middle class women near the factory districts. There I came across the same restlessness as the movie show produced among the wives of the workers in the theatre just now.

"The present psychic condition of India is not at all restful. I came here from New York to find peace. But instead of serenity, whatever I touch stings me with peacelessness. As the poet says, 'Here even the crystal loveliness of the moon has become the dagger-thrust of the sun.' All these years that I have lived in America, I have held the belief that the Indian women can never lose the calm of their soul. Now facts belie my belief. Alas, one must give up one's illusions. This evening I had pinned my hope on the wives of the factory workers. I felt that those who were so poor could not bother to be troubled by anything. I hoped to find in them the age-old serenity of India.

"The funny part of it was that the men whose dominion they resented were slaving nine hours a day in the narrow rooms of the offices to earn twenty-seven dollars, out of which nine went to pay a month's rent. Well, these women were frightfully vociferous and restless. Most appalling. Then their eyes. They were so restless. Our ancient poet spoke of women's bee-black eyes calm as jungle-depths. They are no more calm; they are full of stinging assertiveness. If they only knew what precious things are being sacrificed by them, our women would pause awhile. Kalyana Delei, tell me is freedom worth so much loss of serenity?"

Our feminist friend looked at the sea into whose calm depth the big stars had thrust their long silver maces, while the smaller luminaries had lit innumerable altar fires far and near, uniting sea and sky through a single key of cold light.

"It cannot be arrested now," Mme. Delei said, or seemed to say. "We shall have to find rest beyond and through our unrest. You suffer from too great a desire to arrest the revolt amongst our people. Who can hold back the wind by putting a garland of flowers around its neck? Your words cannot hold the women of India back. At present the iron has entered the soul of our girls. I too have been watching the women's eyes. It is possible for any person to watch them now that they are going about unveiled in such numbers.

"Formerly they looked at you from behind their eyes; now they gaze from the front of their eyes. I know the girls. I am one of them."

Kalyana Delei stopped speaking. She pondered over

what she had said, then added, "Our women are disillusioned. There is no peace in us any more." Then
abruptly, "It is time for you to take me home. . . . I
feel sorry that I took you to that cinema. But then, you
wanted to study the common people."

After we had escorted her to her home, Mr. Earl
and I went to our hotel and sat up all night discussing India.

The substance of my friend's impression I heard just
when the day began to break. He concluded his remarks with these words: "You are carried away by
your fear of unrest. What difference does it make if
one generation of women is sacrificed for the sake of
India's future? I admit I too see unrest. Women do
stare in the manner Mme. Delei described. But I do
not agree that India will lose all of her past."

LETTER III

A NATIONALIST CONFERENCE

LETTER III

A NATIONALIST CONFERENCE

EVER since our arrival some members of the Youth League had persisted in their efforts to make me speak to them. I did my best to avoid any more talking. But Allimir and Mme. Delei were adamant. They insisted that I should speak to the leaders of the movement in private. So one afternoon we met in the house of Mr. Nariman, a lawyer of Bombay. It was in a large room of his enormous house that the meeting was held. About twenty boys and a half a dozen girls—all leaders of different sections of the Youth League—had come armed with questions on America.

Our host, a man of five-and-forty, was a Parsi. Though a lawyer by profession he was preparing to break the Salt Law within a few days' time. In order to profit by the occasion, instead of my answering questions on America, I put a number of them to Mr. Nariman on India. The nostrils of his aquiline nose twitched slightly, like that of a race horse. I asked him to enlighten me on the Salt Law.

After gazing at me with his large eyes, with the air of a bird of prey, Nariman answered, "You know that

salt and the manufacture of it, like opium, is a monopoly of the state. Only the former is an invaluable
blessing, while the latter is a bitter curse. You have also
heard that there is a tax, a high protective tariff on
salt. Thus the poor people of India are forced to buy
salt made by the British government. And if any one
manufactures salt, he is punished by the state. Sometimes men are jailed for a year for having made salt
out of the salt-rocks of Gujrat. A tax on salt exploits
the largest number of Indians who are poor. Since
the Gandhi Movement is a poor people's movement,
we want to knock off the first pair of fetters that binds
them. If thousands of us make salt on our own initi-
ative, the dumb millions will follow our example. In
that way the Salt Act will be made a dead letter though
it may live in the statute book. The situation is somewhat similar to yours before the Revolution when the
British imposed a tax on tea."

It is needless to say here that Mr. Nariman has
broken the Salt Law since and been put in jail with
hundreds of others.

But to continue with our questions. Next I asked
him, "How long can the Nationalist Movement remain
non-violent?"

Mr. Nariman pondered awhile before answering.
Turning to his fellow-workers he said: "It can be
safely predicted that Gandhi's native province, the
province of Gujrat, will practice non-violence to the
bitter end. It is peopled by persons like himself. There

is our Gujrati friend, Mr. Kunshi, who is a brilliant advocate of the High Court, ask him."

Now we turned our gaze to a youthful-looking person. He too was very fair and very aquiline.

Mr. Kunshi needed no pressing. He rubbed his thin hands together a few times, then launched forth. "We of Gujrat have inherited the religion of Ahimso—non-hate and non-violence. For centuries we have returned love for hate in many private quarrels. You remember in 1928 our Bardoli, a district containing eighty thousand people, went on a tax-strike and brought the government to its knees. Non-violent resistance is very congenial to us. But to answer your other question is most difficult. We Gujratis will give a good account of ourselves. Take my case. I am a level-headed lawyer with a decent practice. But I am giving it all up to serve Gandhiji. All the Gujratis will do so. The other provinces will serve him his way as long as he is at large. But our fear is that if he is jailed they may break out into violence. On the contrary in Gujrat we will serve Gandhism in the strictest manner. We must be true to our saint."

"Where does America stand in all this?" asked one of the boys. Apparently he was getting bored with the Gujratis being so holy. At last reluctantly I replied:

"If one can speak for another race, I should think the American people would like to back a purely non-violent revolution." I was interrupted by this question:

"Why shouldn't they back a violent one? Their own

country is founded on a violent revolution. During the last war America did not practice non-violence."

I grew impatient at this youngster. He was very irritating. I said, "You forget Americans too cherish ideals nobler than they can practice during terrible crises. But the fact that they expect us to act nobly in our difficulty is not a slur on their character. Truth to tell, it shows how highly some of them esteem us."

Mr. Nariman and two young lady volunteers agreed with me. But the rest did not know what to make of my statement. One young hopeful reproached America:

"They like to see non-violence in the races that are exploited themselves. Look at Nicaragua."

Here Mr. Earl broke into the conversation. He said, "I do not like our American imperialism. But imperialism or no imperialism—why should you not try non-violence when from the time of Buddha down vast sections of India have practiced it? It is your natural weapon. And if you win through non-violence what a slap that will be in the face of our Western Christian civilization."

They received my friend's words with a strange question. "When will America recognize our independence?"

"First, get your independence," I told him sharply. These young people had begun to annoy me.

Now our host poured oil on troubled water by announcing tea. I was grateful for it. Young people with their crude and abundant vitality should be given plenty to drink.

After tea Mr. Nariman and Mme. Delei took us for a walk on the Chow Pathee Beach. There on the orange sand walked hundreds of girls in their blue, white, green, and purple saris, accompanied by men in long white and blue coats with turbans of citron and green. Even the sun started to spread enchantment on the emerald screen of the sea. Soon the day drooped into darkness. And all the colors fled from the world. But something else very bewitching remained: the people's voices weaving and reweaving their cadences through the gloom.

I shall never forget Chow Pathee Beach for giving me so peaceful an impression of beauty. But why do I drag the name of the beach to your attention? Because here Jawaharlal Nehru, President of our Congress, declared independence January the twenty-sixth, 1930. Chow Pathee is already a national shrine.

But, listen, what is this passing dark wayfarer singing? He is repeating an old lay.

This fever of finding God,
Has made me delirious;
My speech has no meaning,
Yet, I go on speaking.
God, God, God, I repeat, till He bursts out of my soul,
As a river from a rock bounds off to the sea.

LETTER IV

DISENCHANTED EYES

LETTER IV

DISENCHANTED EYES

ALL this time you may be wondering about Kalyana Delei's identity. You know her husband who is a lawyer. Instead of Mr. Delei, it is about her that I should speak. She is more a symbol here than a person. . . .

Her green dress falls on her as folds of her robe fell on the Greek goddess Demeter. Her feet in their brown sandals seem chiselled out of bronze by a Vaskar, god-sculptor. Because she was born and brought up among the rigid Brahmins of the south her movements and gestures have a sense of ritual about them. Her hands she raises and moves from side to side very slowly when she speaks exactly in the manner and rhythm of Arati—waving lit candles before a deity. Similarly her walk; one foot always stretched forward in a straight line from the other as she went on. And when the latter moves, it takes the place of the former exactly fitting into its print, just like a stiletto in its case. Our eyes never tire of watching her. The motion of her body has deep patterns of beauty.

Yet, there is that something about her which marked her apart from the women of the previous generation.

It is the unrest that shines in her eyes. Long lashes, and slightly slanting eyes seem very restless as their gaze moves from object to object with great rapidity. If my friend's wife could only realize that the so-called decorative eyes appear most beautiful when they rest on one thing. Alas, she had no interest in being beautiful just now. All that she wanted was enrolling more soldiers for Gandhi's militia of passive resistance.

Kalyana Delei, like many modern girls, married whom she chose and not the one chosen for her. She lives her life as she pleases. That is why she is in politics now.

It was at luncheon, our second day in Bombay, that I unburdened my soul before Mme. Delei, "Kalyana, my dear old friend, your husband is making a great mistake by aiding and abetting you in your revolutionary work. You are losing your culture. The beautiful culture of our ancestors will be lost if you girls go on like this. My mother used to say, 'Woman must live by necessity.' Our modern Hindu girl wants to live for self-expression.

"I doubt if this is good for her spirit. I doubt gravely the whole trend of our women's life. It was bad enough to have made them conscious of their wrongs. Now we are helping them to revolt and fight, for what? Is it all for the best?"

Kalyana grew animated to the point of being peevish as she spoke: "What matters today is not our girls being disenchanted, but their accepting the British as the best model of progress in the world. Foreign domination means our imitating foreign models."

"But must you fight the devil with fire? In order to fight the British you are making yourselves hopelessly unsettled. Our women used to be so tranquil and so profound. Now they are only clever and uneasy," I said with some force.

My friend's wife now spoke words of reason. "It cannot be denied that we are really acquiring a philosophy of personal happiness. Our girls are no more willing to live by necessity and its most purifying process. Formerly they accepted peacefully love, marriage, child-bearing and death as gifts from necessity. Each and every good and evil experience they met with the fortitude of a deity. Nowadays we boil with indignation if someone inflicts any injury upon us. The older Hindu woman never cried out in pain when going through the birth-pangs. Never! But our generation—you ought to hear us." Then Kalyana laughed, showing her 'jasmin-white teeth,' as the Bengali poet puts it.

"So, you have learned to personalize suffering," I mused aloud. "Were you taught that way by your parents?"

"Oh, no!" Kalyana exclaimed, her eyes flashing. . . . "I was taught words of great wisdom. My mother repeated with different phrases this one central truth: 'She alone is wise who lives by necessity. Nimitta matra—become as a chisel in the hand of God.' " After a pause she went on reminiscently: "How I remember my Brahmin father of the old school saying to me at the age of nine, when I had cut my finger badly peeling potatoes, 'Daughter, no woman should say that *she* is hurt. You must learn to say that hurt is.' No woman of my generation was encouraged to personalize her pain. Now we have begun. It may annoy you. But I prefer saying, 'I suffer,' instead of mumbling 'suffering is.'"

"I do not approve of it," I said with a touch of finality. "Personality came into Europe with Rousseau and the damnable Romanticists. It, like the idea of progress, is a very young delusion. Why get caught in either? Romanticism gives us the most theatrical experiences in the place of the truly dramatic. Soon, you, the noblest of women, will go in for thrills. Yes, the whole tribe of you. I can foresee the degeneracy that is lying in wait for our Hindu womanhood. Why can you not free yourselves without swallowing the fraudulent philosophy of romantic freedom? Can you not do simple acts without a complex doctrine? Soon every one of life's vivid experiences will be sacrificed for a thrilling one. Each woman will proclaim through books and stories, 'Behold my crucified life!' And the gods will answer back, 'You are not crucified, because you have never lived. True living is such a genuine kind of self-destruction that no self can speak of it.'

"What is this necessity that the Indian woman is

relinquishing? Let me answer it from the realm of fiction. It is that sense of elemental verity that made Antigone, 'go uphill in the tainted air of the noon in order to throw a handful of dust on her brother's corpse that had no tomb.' It is the same sense that made Alkestis give her life as a ransom for the one who loved life more than she. Nothing but necessity caused Penelope to deceive her suitors with the long meshes wrought and unwrought by her unresting needles of steel. I can go still further and speak of women from the Hindu epics. Sita, Savitri, Damayanti, Gandhari, and others, all lived by that law old as God— necessity. They knew how to eschew the possible, and how to will the inevitable.

"Now that our ancient sense of necessity is leaving our women, on what foundations shall we erect our culture? Kasmai, Devaya, Havisha, Vidhema—to what god shall we offer sacrifice today? Your future is perilous. A race that makes its women restless lives not by the verities. Instead, it shall perish through lies. Only a solid foundation of soul-peace builds culture. Now that we are throwing away our culture, what will save us in our hour of spiritual trial?"

Without meditating awhile on the grave words of wisdom uttered by myself, Kalyana Delei leaned forward a little and said, "Ice cream for dessert?"

Thank God for my sense of humour. I took the levity of her remark as it was meant to be.

"Look," she called my attention, "here is my husband. It is a pity he did not hear you during the past ten minutes. You were most eloquent."

Since this is a letter devoted to the new woman of India, I shall not say anything here about the new woman's husband. What do you think had brought Kalyana's husband to the hotel dining-room? He had had a business luncheon with Sir George, an English lawyer, regarding 'a case.' And now he had come to take his wife and me to a women's meeting in the slums near Parel. Thither we went in their Minerva car. During our journey, I went on telling Kalyana Delei some more about the ancient wisdom of India and the delusions of modern romanticism. I am afraid I wasted my breath.

LETTER V

BAZARS

LETTER V

BAZARS

I AM afraid I talked too much about Indian women in my last letter. Permit me to draw a picture of the bazars of Bombay in this one.

Can you visualize an ugly, modern city of factory chimneys made unbearable by mediocre efforts at city-beautifying? Bombay would be a grand sight if its factories were allowed to speak for it. Instead, many second-rate imitations of the so-called artistic buildings of Europe of the Nineteenth Century have been placed here for the sake of redeeming its ugliness.

People do not realize that there is beauty in factory chimneys. Every time one goes by Gary, Indiana, one is impressed by its grotesque grandeur. Gary, at night, reminds one of Vulcan's forge. The human spirit is never debased by such a sight. For it is not mediocre. If Bombay were left desolate with ugliness and fiercely fuming factory chimneys, it would startle any visitor with its divine horrors. There would be a touch of genius about it.

Alas, some foolish patrons of the arts, hesitating to let the city alone, set about beautifying Bombay. Hence its art museum, its large hotels, public gardens, hospitals, and lifeless statues: all solemnly mediocre.

Unable to bear the sight of them any longer, we decided to spend our last day in the bazars, where oriental manners reign supreme. About six in the morning, we set out. The city had just begun to wake up. A Papia, Indian lark, sang his salutation to the risen sun from a mango tree of the hotel garden. Crows cawed with rapture as they drew their tattered black sails over yellow and rose-red roofs. Far off shrilly whistled the kites. But above them one heard the roar of many factories calling their toilers to work.

In the streets as we neared the bazars rose the odor of frankincense, signifying that the Marwari, a class of money-changers, were praying to Lakshimi, the Hindu Fortuna, for abundant good fortune during the forthcoming business hours. Further on, the flute-blowers from the front tower of a large temple were pouring their orison tone by tone, cadenza upon cadenza, against the noise and tumult of the risen city.

At this point the odor of mango seized my nostrils. I forgot all about Bombay. Off we went to the mango booths. Its fragrance, like crushed strawberries and roses, ascends to heaven. Around carmine mountains of piled mangoes, vendors in green and russet chanted and yelled the virtues of their goods. "Ohe, mine are just ripe like a damsel for her nuptial kiss." "Ohe," piped another, "its skin is smooth like enamel, only one dollar for five pounds." There was another who seemed to howl with joy: "My mangoes are precious as

Mohurs and Asrafi, royal gold and imperial medallion. Taste one and it will wipe out all your worst memories. These are not mangoes, they are nectar. Taste and see! Four pounds for three rupees."

Far off in a corner sat a graybeard with a basket of fruits. "What are you selling, Baba, father?" I asked him.

"Amrai, mangoes, my son," he answered in a voice almost feeble.

"Why don't you sing the praise of your goods?" Mr. Earl wanted to know.

The old man's brown eyes grew bright with mischief. He said, "How can a poet sing when donkeys bray lustily? Though I shout not, I shall sell half of my burden before they get rid of a quarter of their merchandise. Only fools think that screaming is a part of salesmanship. . . . How many mangoes shall I sell thee?"

Mr. Earl hesitated to say anything. But that got him into the old man's trap all the deeper. He said, "I shall sell thee a dozen. Four for madame, four for the miss, and four for the master of the house."

I said, "Well, he knows how many souls make your family. The old wizard!"

Here the mango-vendor turned to me saying, "Tell him two rupees—not a penny less."

More with the gesture of one who gives than one who receives money, the ancient rascal held out his hand for two pieces of silver. In order to meet it with an equal air of grandeur my friend gave him the rupees. After putting them in his leather sack the Amrai-wallah announced, "Give me your address, the fruits will reach there before yourselves."

"What a salesman!" we exclaimed as we left the mango-booths.

The most beautiful sight in the markets of Bombay is that of the flower section. At half-past six, blossoms of champak and jasmin, hibiscus, yellow sal, oleanders, white syringas, blue lilies, and scarlet roses are massed like a forest of fragrance. And their beauty grew all the more poignant, for one knew only too well that the hot sun of the tropics would scorch and kill each one of them before ten o'clock. Beauty is brief where life is abundant.

The flower-vendors did not scream in order to sell their merchandise. Knowing that those who love flowers know what they want, their sellers never clamour much. But do not for a moment infer that they do not talk. Alas, my friend, all Hindus are tremendous talkers. Like the Greeks, "the gods created" the Hindus "for conversation."

Noticing a beautiful big rose just drooping, I asked its vendor, "Why not give it some water?"

He answered, "It has water, O little mister. But every drop of water is warm by now. The sun is too strong. But the rose is like a woman, having resistance and wisdom."

"What is the wisdom of a rose?" inquired Earl.

The merchant recited this poem in answer:

"In the city of Ghazipore, where rose water is manufac-
tured, I wandered into the house of a perfume-maker.
There on a fire I beheld a large vat slowly steaming.
It was filled with white flowers on whom like a diadem
was set a large red rose which was turning white
petal by petal.
I said to the pain-laden one, 'O rose, why must you suffer
so?'
It answered, 'Do you not see that I must pay for what I
have done?
I must die thus, for having dared to smile in a desert."

From the flower booths I wanted to go to the shoe-
merchants, jooti-wallas. But Mr. Earl decided to do
no shopping there. So we went to the brocade-dealers.
Here was something to delight the heart of a con-
noisseur. Silk, like a lovely language spoken by a pure
voice, quickened our hearts. "One does not touch silk,
one hears it," the saying goes.

Alas, there was a thorn in this blossom. The modern Benares silk, or any other, say the silk of Assam,
is embroidered with designs sent from London, New
York, and Berlin. The weavers must work them, for
they must sell their handiwork to Western houses.
Though the new designs cannot be sung, nor cursed,
the greater part of them appears to our old eyes as a
sort of scandal. We asked one dealer the reason for
the popularity of these designs.

He answered, "In India since the war taste is dying.
People cannot understand a design of cedars wrought

in gold on the borders of a purple fabric which looks like Amrit Ka Sar—the lake of Ambrosia at twilight. They want antelopes jumping around the edge of their garments. Or, monkeys moving from branch to branch. What can we do but supply the animals to their kin?"

"Where can we find the old?" asked Mr. Earl.

"You will find the old designs in the second-hand shops, just 'round the corner," we were informed.

So thither we went. And the gods were good to us. For a mere song my friend picked up silk fabrics fifty years old whose workmanship is priceless. A very tall, ugly vendor, full of hair on his face like a superannuated lion, sat surrounded with silk of Assam, Benares, Bhagalpore, Prayaga, and Shrinagar. The word rainbow cannot begin to describe the kinds of silk that lay heaped about him. This vendor had eyes like an owl's, half closed all day long.

But I shall not describe him. For what matters to you and me is the story he told. He brought out an old sandalwood chest and opened it. Out of it emerged a gold-tissue dress of the early Eighteenth Century. Green cloth with tissues of gold, that is what it was. The man permitted us to feel the texture of the fabric.

He kept saying, "This one sings every time you touch it. It belonged to a Mogul nobleman before 1857. Then came the revolution. The British wiped out the Moguls. The owner of this garment pawned everything from time to time. Last of all he pawned this in the eighties to my father. . . . You perceive the design—sunset in the green pastures of the spring-stung north. I can sing the design to you. 'Here the green is lush as brook-fed grass, and hard as tempered steel. Threads of gold, like arteries from the body of the sun.' " He interrupted his song in order to explain further: "Every turn of the gold, every circle and even the littlest form were sung. In those days designs were taught by word of mouth from father to son. Even now if they have an old design to weave and embroider they never draw the design on paper—they pull it out of their heads, chanting verse by verse as a snake charmer pulls the hooded cobra out of his hole by fluting to it. I shall sing of this fabric to you." Now he resumed his song. After a half hour of singing he stopped. I was startled by a sudden noise of applause.

A crowd had gathered about his booth, intently watching the singer, and the American gentleman listening with his mouth open. Now the question of buying something arose. We had not money enough to buy the work of gold-tissue, we informed the shop-keeper. He did not mind at all. He was glad to meet someone that liked old fabrics.

LETTER VI

JAWAHARLAL OF ALLAHABAD

LETTER VI

JAWAHARLAL NEHRU OF ALLAHABAD

FROM Bombay we went to Allahabad where the Kumbha Mela was coming to its end. But our reason for going there was twofold. For it was the town of Nehru, President of the Indian Congress, and it was exactly halfway between Bombay and Calcutta.

Would it be too much if I try to describe briefly a twilight on the plains of northern India before our train pulled into Prayaga, Allahabad? I would not have thought of it were it not for Mr. Earl's insistence. He said, "This is uniquely Indian. It cannot happen anywhere else. This soil speaks at this hour. The soil is more important than her sons, like Buddha, Asoka, Aklar, Shah Jehan, and Mahatma Gandhi."

Though our train thundered on, it could not mar the stillness of the countryside. The brown fields deepening into dark, the mango trees rising like fountains of jet against the lilac horizon, and the silent cattle, all seemed to speak of a divine presence. An unspeakable pain seemed to mingle with a sense of release. More than four thousand years of history augmented its human significance. The landscape grew ashen now. Untold generations of Hindus had been buried or cre-

71

mated here. Their memory spread its bloom of silver over each thing. The moon had risen. The short tropical twilight had passed swiftly. The whole world, vestured in peace, knelt at the feet of night.

But India is a country of anticlimax. Without giving any notice, our train stopped suddenly. A white-robed figure, in a green turban large as a basket, told us in stentorian tones, "This is the station for you to get off in order to walk to the dining car, sir."

Mr. Earl said indignantly in French, "Imbeciles! Can we not eat another time? Why must they eat just now?"

The turbaned figure who had understood the English words responded, "It is your only chance to dine before Allahabad, which is the next station. Exactly an hour."

We had to follow the Ardali, waiter, to the dining car which blazed with many electric lights. Englishmen and Hindus were solemnly cultivating gastronomy. I joined them with pleasure; for every occasion that gives me a spiritual and aesthetic joy leaves me hungry as a wolf. What a keen insight into human nature Richard Wagner displayed when he provided shops of sandwiches and beer near his playhouse in Bayreuth.

When we reached Prayaga, our train was met by Jawaharlal Nehru. Though twenty years younger than Gandhi, Jawaharlal resembles the master in more ways

than one. His head has exactly the same high and
well-rounded doming as has Gandhi's. From behind
his eyes he pours forth an undimmed light of friend-
liness. The only thing fierce about him is his mouth.
Its corners have hardened considerably since the police
beat Jawaharlal with large sticks when he led a procession of non-violent boycotters to the Simon Commission a year ago.

On reaching the Nehru home he took off his cap.
I was startled to see that every hair of his head had
turned white. "At last," I informed myself, "he has
earned his old age. He is free of all delusions of the
self. In him Gandhi has forged a thunderbolt. Now it
is safe to predict that India will be freed in less than
a quarter of a century. Here is her Garibaldi and
Cavour rolled in one."

It would interest you to know why I use the example of Italy in order to explain modern India. India
occupies the same position in the map of Asia as does
Italy in Europe. India of the Gupta Empire was great
at the time when the Augustan Empire of Rome had
become stable. Later both of them suffered barbarian
invasions. Savages poured into Rome through the
passes of the Alps, as the Arabs and Mongols streamed
into Hindustan through the Khyber and the Bolun.

If the Holy Roman Empire brought some peace to
distracted Italy so did the Rajput autocracy in India.
Italy lived on under Germanic dynasties, while India
lived on under Mohammedan empires that ruled

peacefully for a hundred years or so and then collapsed. At last came the glorious age of the Popes of the Renaissance to Italy, and so came the Mogul Empire in India. Art flourished from the time of Akbar to Aurangzeb about a hundred and fifty years in our country, where Europe sought a sea-route not for philanthropy but for making money. Poets like Marlowe sang of flying "to India for gold." Milton reached a fabulous comparison when he spoke of "wealth that surpassed that of Ormuz and Ind." In the age of the English Puritans Italy stod as a symbol of learning and art, as did India symbolize art and wealth.

Then came the evil days. The mercenary policy of the Austrian monarchy and the Italian nobles ruined Italy during the Eighteenth Century. The same thing happened to India through the exploitation of the decaying Moguls and the British East India Company.

Fortunately for Italy she was roused by Mazzini about seventy years ago. India's awakening has come through Gandhi. Italy is free and forging ahead to build a new Roman Empire. India too will parallel her, not through conquest, but through the gifts of her spirit.

What concrete evidence have I that proves "beyond any reasonable doubt" that India is treading the new orbit of freedom? My knowledge of Indian languages, my penetration into our people's mind, and the facts before my eyes speak loudly. "You will be free soon, for your people are growing in courage," I seem to hear from the very soil. At railway stations, in bazars, in every public place where the common Indian comes in direct contact with the British the son of our soil does not cringe. He is not afraid to rub shoulders with the Briton with perfect ease. The other day at the station of Bhoom an Englishman started to say something unpleasant to a porter. But halfway through his sentence he checked himself. Whether he acted prudently, or was obeying the recent instructions of his superiors, it betokens the fact that the British too are aware of the new spirit born in all of us. They do not like to annoy us as they used to. We are no more a diseased race. We have grown normal and strong. We are healed of fear. This healing we owe to Gandhi first, and Jawaharlal next. I never dreamt that such a miracle would come to pass in my lifetime. Now it does not matter whether it takes two or twenty years to free the nation. The health of the spirit that liberates a people is acting like a leaven in Hindustan.

LETTER VII

POLITICAL DISILLUSION

LETTER VII

POLITICAL DISILLUSION

THE next morning at about five the papia, the Indian lark, the saris, the martens, the kokila, and the cuckoo sang so lustily that they awoke the whole world. The daybreak had shed light like dust made out of mother-of-pearl. In it the mango trees dripped with silver; the acacias and the tamarind were etched like herds of elephants against the morning sky.

Jawaharlal, finding sleep out of the question, invited me to partake of his tea on the veranda, that ran like a terrace around the whole house.

Like a bustling reporter I said to him, "Look here, while my American friend is meditating, I want to ask you a few academic questions. First of all, tell me why you people have been so distrustful of every political concession that the British have made? Can you tell me the whole history?"

Nehru laughed. "You remind me of the two American Christian ministers who came here six weeks ago. They asked me point blank if I had experienced God. Of course, that would be an easier question to ask than to answer. Fortunately, your question is not so very difficult."

"I am questioning you, because according to the British, and some Americans, it was you who spurned the Viceroy's proposal of a Round Table Conference with the British," I made myself clear. "Wasn't it in November last?"

Nehru smiled. "They exaggerate. It was Gandhi who agreed to spurn it. The only way to make you see it, is to deal with the whole business historically. I shall begin with the year 1917 when the British Parliament promised us responsible self-government in exchange for the help India had given in money and men during the war. At that time Gandhi contradicted his philosophy of non-violence in order to recruit troops for the British throughout India. All of us trusted the British. Their promise was a sacred bond.

"No sooner had the war been over than they began to go back on their word of honour. They kept on the statute book the most reactionary war-time measures, including the right to arrest and imprison people without any trial. Next, they gave us a bastard political constitution which sanctioned the complete control of the portfolios of finance, the police, the army, and the foreign consulates to a British oligarchy above all legislatures, and permitted us to have the portfolios of education and sanitation. You cannot do anything for education when the Hindu minister of education must beg of the English minister of finance for money at every turn.

"Thus the constitution proved to be a deception. As if that were not enough; on top of it the Amritsar Massacre of 1919 took place. Now Gandhi who had been a helper of the British for nearly a quarter of a century was completely disillusioned. He embarked upon his policy of non-violent non-cooperation. I worked under him, and went to jail along with forty thousand others. Gandhi too was imprisoned. And eventually our movement was successfully crushed. All this was done by our Jewish Viceroy, Lord Reading, whose genius should not be underestimated.

"Between 1922 and 1928 the deceptive Montague Chelmsford constitution was kept in force. Then the British Parliament sent us the Simon Commission, consisting solely of Britishers, to examine our fitness for further advance in constitutional government. We knew it to be nothing but another fraud. This time, unlike 1918–1919, not only we, the Indian Congress Party, but even the privileged classes, such as the Moderates and the Liberal Party, boycotted it. None of us would go near it. But we of the Congress went further. We paraded the streets with black flags and with placards saying, 'Simon, Go Back.'

"When the six Britons headed by Sir John Simon came to Lucknow, the capital of our province (the United Provinces), many of my friends and I went to greet them with black flags. But the police would not let us go near the Commission. Though we were totally unarmed we were bludgeoned most severely. Anyway, the Simon Commission did not have a very friendly reception everywhere.

"The situation had grown so aggravated by the spring of 1929 that the Viceroy had to go to Great Britain to talk things over with the Labor Cabinet. In order to save the face of the Simon Commission and of his own regime, on his return from England, November, 1929, Lord Irwin made the famous offer of a Round Table Conference between some representatives of the British Parliament and of the Indian Political Parties. What is the Round Table Conference to do? It is to negotiate on the basis of the findings of the Simon Commission a constitution for India which will definitely set down India's final goal to be a status like that of Canada within the British Empire. 'Oh, the inextinguishable laughter of the gods!' India's final destiny to be a self-governing dominion like South Africa! Can you surpass such a piece of imaginative fiction? India, according to the British, though she has lived forty centuries without hearing of Great Britain, cannot have any destiny apart from the British Empire. Koota Ajata, Kootaiam Bishristi—how has this come about, whence such a creation?'

"Gandhi, the very soul of generosity, went to see the Viceroy. He was willing to meet the Round Table Conference if, as a proof of its good will, Lord Irwin's government were willing to grant an amnesty to all political prisoners. I knew all along that nothing would come of it. Gandhiji could get no practical concession of any kind from the government. In the past years it has broken so many promises that without some tangible objective move on its part, we could put no faith in any oral proposal offered by the present regime. We can trust facts but not words.

"We waited 'til December 31, 1929, and then proclaimed to the world that India's final goal is not to be a part of the Empire, but to be completely herself without being tied to any other nation on earth. Gandhi who had been deeply disillusioned by now began to think out a practical form of resistance to the present regime. Suddenly he has hit upon the Salt Tax. The government must be made to lift the tax on salt, and it must also give up its salt monopoly. The campaign has begun. Gandhi makes salt the day after tomorrow. Then I will make it here. You can go back and tell your friends that India is completely disillusioned. She places no faith in external saviors."

By now it was seven o'clock. Mr. Earl had not only finished his meditations, but had softly walked near us and had heard the last few sentences from Nehru.

"Too bad," he exclaimed, "I was meditating. I must have missed something."

At this point I questioned Nehru about the possibility of a violent revolution in India. "Is there a well-organized party of violence who are planning to plunge our country into chaos?"

Nehru had to admit that there was a Violence Party.

"But I think," he went on, "one does not know how well organized they are, since they do everything in secret. If they ever get the upper hand, India will be in ruins. Fearing that they may gain the upper hand, Gandhi and the 'Congress Party' deemed it wise to launch the present non-violent revolution. The people are so restive that if we do not give them any lead they will be incited into violence.

"Well, we have begun. No man can prophesy as to the outcome of the present struggle. If India wins without violence her revolution will not be followed by a civil war which seems to follow all violent revolutions. I am against every kind of violence. My firm belief is that we have launched the Gandhi movement just in the nick of time."

"You know, Mr. Nehru," Earl spoke his mind, "the way you put things is somewhat blunt. I do not think any American will be seduced into taking your part after he reads what you have just said. Can you not put the matter differently?"

Nehru smiled for an instant before his lips tightened. With an expression of sadness that spread over his face he spoke: "I am not a man of words; action is my forte. Anyway, I hold that India can be freed only by action here and not through writing books in America."

In order not to lose any chance I now trotted out the question many American gentlemen have asked me: "Why can you not accept Dominion Status in the place of complete separation from England?"

Nehru shut his eyes for a few seconds. After carefully thinking over his speech he began, his face blazing with enthusiasm: "But how can we accept Dominion Status when it has not been offered us by Ramsay MacDonald's government? Do you not see that the Viceroy says nothing about our attaining immediate Dominion Status? What he does say is that a constitution will be drafted next October at the Round Table Conference which will set forth the fact that India's ultimate status will be that of a dominion in the British Commonwealth of Nations. Nowhere in his utterances do I find even the remotest hint that he is offering India immediate dominion government.

"I personally believe that England cannot grant India the status of a dominion. I have very good reason for this belief; she can't afford it."

"How is that?" Mr. Earl and I asked in unison.

For a few moments Nehru laughed at us. "The reason that I have in mind is very simple. Let us assume that Great Britain, Canada, Australia, South Africa and New Zealand—all put together have a population of one hundred and ten million people who are not of our race and tradition. What would happen to them if all of a sudden these people were brought face to face with three hundred and twenty million Indians made their political equal through Dominion Status?

Can't you see that we as a majority will dictate to them? Instead of British it will be an Indian Empire.

"Now let me ask you this: have you noticed the character of the British men and women who talk of India's being made equal to the dominions? They are generally members of the Labor Party. You will not find many conservatives talking such pietistic froth. The latter have thought imperially for years, along with governing the empire. They are realists because they know India. They are quite sure that India as a dominion instead of solving any problem will become a very thorny issue for the empire. Have you ever heard many members of the Conservative Party talk of giving India full Dominion Status? They never do.

"The reason for the Labor Party's pledging to give India equality with the dominions lies in its ignorance of the problem. Not having studied India and the imperial problems as thoroughly as the Tories, they sail where angels fear to tread. And when it comes to holding India down during any crisis, mark my words, the present Labor cabinet will commit more blunders and atrocities than any other that had to tackle a similar job. They will talk of Dominion Status for India with their lips while their hands will be busy shooting down unarmed men and women. That is what comes of handing over an empire to ill-informed pious men.

"Now take the Tories who have studied the rudi-

ments of the Indian problem—they know some facts—
they would rather see India cut off from the Empire
than give her equality with the rest of the dominions.
It is because they knew more than the Labor Party;
the cabinet that settled the Egyptian issue did not make
Egypt a dominion. Instead they granted it independence—at least on paper. Now, behold, the Egyptians
have to make the best of it. Though Ramsay Mac-
Donald talks of peace and brotherliness he cannot offer
the Egyptians more than his predecessors. Here too
labor talks pacifism but acts war.

"I do not for a moment believe that Labor will
grant India Dominion Status at the Round Table Conference next October. That is why our present Viceroy could not pledge Gandhi last December anything
beyond the hope that at the Conference a constitution
will be made which will settle India's ultimate status
as a dominion. Despite all its talk, the Labor Party
can do nothing more for India.

"Now I shall give you a forecast of the utmost concession that the British will make at the Conference.
Their final offer will give India equality of status with
the dominions provided the Indian Army, the Police,
the Consular, and the Immigration services are left in
British control. This can't satisfy us.

"You see if we control our immigration and army
we would surely demand Canada, Australia, and South
Africa to permit free Indian immigration in those
countries besides enfranchising and equalizing the

status of each immigrant. Can you imagine our fellow-dominions in such a mess? Can any man in his senses ever think of the dominions complying with any such demand?

"On the contrary, if India were free, as Japan is free, she could not ask for free immigration. Japan, though independent, cannot get equal rights for her emigrating subjects in many foreign countries. India independent is less of a problem.

"You see that as a full-fledged dominion, India could act worse than Japan. That is why in order to prevent her obtaining the real thing she will be given a qualified Dominion Status. She will be permitted to call herself a dominion, but will not be given all the rights of one. She will have the status but not the strength of an equal. There will be no Indian control of her army, police, and diplomatic services.

"If we demand complete control of our army, and couple it with a demand for having our own consulates and immigration services abroad, all the three British political parties will unite in a common opposition to us. They would rather fight than concede any such demands. Even Dominion Status cannot be had without a war. Since we have to fight, I do not see why we should spill our blood for Dominion Status. Even a non-violent army should fight for the largest end possible. Independence should be the goal of men who are about to die for their country. I hope I have explained to you why I stand for independence."

"Is there no way of inducing you to go to the Round Table Conference?" I begged for an answer.

Jawaharlal's brows wrinkled and the corners of his mouth hardened like that of a statue. Apparently he considered the Conference not worth discussing. But some idea in the hinterland of his mind made him say this: "It might be worth attending if the British invite our people to erect a machinery for the immediate working of full Dominion Status. This they will not do until later, much later. In the meantime why anyone should go to London to discuss dominion without status, or status without dominion, passes my understanding."

LETTER VIII

WHAT THE OFFICIAL BRITISH MIND BELIEVES

LETTER VIII

WHAT THE OFFICIAL BRITISH MIND BELIEVES

SOME philosophers maintain that the tragic events issue from a conflict, not of right and wrong, but of right against right. President Nehru's statement will tell you how right he is. Now I shall quote what his opponent, the upright Britisher like the present Viceroy, Lord Irwin, thinks. If you look into his mind, you will find that he too believes himself to be in the right. Permit me to quote the Viceroy's statement:

"At this juncture of India's history I desire to recall the attention of her people to the main facts out of which the present situation has developed.

"On November 1, last, I made an announcement on behalf of his Majesty's Government that, in their judgment, it was implicit in the Declaration of 1917 that the natural issue of India's constitutional progress as there contemplated was the attainment of Dominion Status. I further stated that when the Statutory Commission and the Indian Central Committee had submitted their Reports, and these had been published, and when his Majesty's Government had been able, in consultation with the Government of India, to consider these matters in the light of all the material then available, they would propose to invite representatives of the different parties and interests in British India and representatives of the Indian States to meet them, separately or together as circumstances might demand, for the purpose of conference and discussion in regard to both British India and the All-India problems.

"On December 23, when I met Mr. Gandhi and Pandit Motilal Nehru, they made it plain that they were not prepared to participate in the Conference except upon new conditions which had found no place in my announcement, and, consequent upon this, the Congress at Lahore, under the guidance of Mr. Gandhi, proclaimed its creed to be that of complete independence. It is matter for great regret that anybody of Indian opinion should have rejected the offer of his Majesty's Government. As I have said on a previous occasion, those who have so acted have spurned an opportunity unprecedented in India's history, and have rejected a unique chance of playing a constructive part in the evolution of India's future. In order to defeat the proposal of his Majesty's Government, they have sought to proceed not by constitutional means, as might have been expected to appeal to reasonable men, but have deliberately embarked upon a course of civil disobedience fraught with dangers to which it is impossible to suppose its authors can any longer be blind.

"In pursuance of the Congress resolution, Mr. Gandhi sent me on March 2, last, a letter, which has been given wide publicity, announcing his intention to institute his campaign of civil disobedience on March 11 by proceeding to disregard the provisions of the Salt Laws. He explained his decision on the ground that the party of violence was gaining strength, that he had an unquestioning and immovable faith in the efficacy of non-violence to be expressed through civil disobedience, and that it would therefore be sinful on his part to wait longer. He concluded by admitting the knowledge that in embarking on non-violence he would be running what might fairly be termed a mad risk. In the reply which I caused to be sent to his letter my regret was expressed that he contemplated a course of action which was clearly bound to involve a violation of the law and a danger to public peace.

"In my last address to the Legislative Assembly on January 25 I was at pains to make clear the inevitable consequences of the adoption of unconstitutional and unlawful methods to bring about political changes, to which Mr. Gandhi and his followers stood committed. I further made it plain that, while it remained my firm desire, as it was that of his Majesty's Government, to do everything possible for conciliation in order that Great Britain and India might collaborate together in finding a solution of our present difficulties, it was no less incumbent upon myself and my Government to discharge our responsibility for the effective maintenance of the law's authority and for the preservation of peace and order.

"The events of the past three weeks have been a melancholy fulfilment of the anticipation expressed in my reply to Mr. Gandhi's letter. From quarters as far distant as Peshawar and Madras, Bombay and Calcutta, Chittagong and Karachi, Delhi and Sholapur, have come ominous tales of mob violence, of armed and murderous raid, and of general defiance of lawful authority. With regret, but inevitably, my Government have been compelled, in face of this growing menace to the well-being and security of the Indian public, to arm themselves and the Provincial Governments with such further weapons as we judged necessary and expedient to restore in the eyes of the world the good name of India for sanity and respect for constituted authority. Driven, as I and my Government have been, by force of circumstances and by the action of others to take these steps (and I hope that wiser counsels may soon prevail which may render unnecessary the continuance of the measures designed to meet an emergency), I desire to make it plain that our purpose remains unchanged, and that neither my Government nor his Majesty's Government will be deflected by these unhappy events from our firm determination to abide by the policy I was privileged to announce on behalf of his Majesty's Government on November 1, last. Steps are being actively taken to arrange for the assembling in London representatives at the Conference there contemplated on or about October 20, next. Though this date is later than in some respects I could have wished, it will offer the advantage to the delegates from India of establishing personal relations with Dominion representatives, who will then be present in London in connection with the Imperial Conference, which has already been arranged to meet at the end of September. The actual opening of the Indian Conference would follow immediately the conclusion of the Imperial Conference.

"If I may sound a more personal note, I would say that those who know my mind best will realize how great is the store which I set upon the outcome of this policy. But constructive work such as that which we are eager to begin is only prejudiced and obstructed by disorder. I would accordingly appeal to all persons throughout India calmly and dispassionately to consider these facts for themselves. I recognize that at the present time there is a widespread desire throughout India to see real political advance, and I have learnt to love India too well to relax any effort to assist what I hold to be the natural and true development of her political life. Such development depends upon the solution of real problems, among which there is none more important than that which affects the future position of the authorities. So far as this is concerned, it is evident that no settlement can be considered satisfactory which does not carry the consent of, and give a sense of security to, the important minority communities who will have to live under the new Constitution. But so long as those responsible for the civil disobedience movement refuse to recognize realities, and proceed as if all that was necessary was to break the law, regardless of the consequences such action must entail, so long will they be postponing the very thing that they profess to desire for India, and that others, who do not share their reluctance to see facts as they are, might by this time have gone far to achieve. No more severe condemnation has ever been passed upon any persons than that in which it was said of some that they entered not in themselves and them that were entering in they hindered."—Irwin.

LETTER IX

KUMBHA-MELA
A LEGACY OF OUR RELIGIOUS PAST

LETTER IX

KUMBHA-MELA, A LEGACY OF OUR RELIGIOUS PAST

ALL the Nehrus told me that I should have arrived two weeks earlier to see the Kumbha festivals at their peak. "Now," they informed me, "you will see its very frail declining. Nothing is there to indicate what it has been."

But what I beheld was sumptuous enough. From it I could easily imagine the Mela, festival, at its most picturesque. I felt as if the whole drama was being enacted before my very eyes. . . .

Between yellow sandstone walls, walking down enormous steps, the pilgrims descend into the ebony waters of the Tribeni—the three rivers. Women in violet robes throng against men in pure white, and above them stand princes and rajas in purple and orange and amber. On the topmost steps half-naked holy men ride on white stallions, and in the streets beyond innumerable elephants, caparisoned in cloth of gold, walk softly as mice.

It is the Kumbha-Mela, the mighty religious festival that takes place in Allahabad once every fourteen years. The moon of December has waned, the January moon has begun to wax, and today, January 5, inaugurates the holiest period of the moon. Allahabad is especially holy because here all the three rivers meet. It is here that more than 4,000,000 people were expected to bathe during the festival.

Legend says that the three rivers—the Ganges, the Jumna and the underground Saraswati—are named after the three daughters of the mighty King Himalaya, lord of the mightiest mountains in the world. When these three daughters had left their father to go to the sea they became so homesick that he arranged to have them meet again and he chose as their meeting place Allahabad. So there, once every fourteen years, the underground Saraswati comes up to see her sisters. (The observant say they can even see the bubbles.) The three talk of their father vestured in cloud and seated in the heavens, while any one bathing in their waters is purified of his sins. And if one bathes at Allahabad, where they all meet, one is doubly purified.

For centuries and centuries this Kumbha-Mela has been celebrated. There are many ballads of the eleventh century commemorating it. The inference is that it goes back to the remotest antiquity, for Valmiki, the Hindu Homer, wrote of significant events around Allahabad in his epic, the Ramayana. And for thousands of years Hindus have called this city (where the two rivers, the Ganges and the Jumna, are locked in a single embrace and where their third sister periodically joins them for a rendezvous) Prayaga, or the City of God.

One of the rivers is a tawny yellow and the other is dark as ebony, but when a woman or a man clad in crimson or in emerald dips into the water the colors break into a thousand running bits of liquid splendor.

The water is cruelly cold, but the people do not notice that. They are not concentrating on their physical comfort, they are concentrating on a thought. If you go to one of the holy men sitting under a tree, or one, naked to the waist, sitting astride a milk-white stallion, he will explain this to you. He will say to you, quietly:

"People do not come to bathe in the water here. They come to bathe in a thought. This thought, we and our disciples and millions of others are holding throughout India: 'O God! Cleanse us of hate and fear. Cleanse each soul of unrest. May every pilgrim return home burning with peace and love. May each one carry in himself, as in a kumbha (water-pitcher), perfect purity that will not be exhausted for years to come.' Every soul is filled like a pitcher with the essence of God."

Brahmins in their robes of ochre silk and untouchable pariahs in their topaz gowns, caste forgotten in the ecstasy of the hour, all bathe in the water.

Each person's face is illumined by devotion. People from all over India are here in the dark interior of the temple, golden with candle flames. Here are Bengalis in white and scarlet robes, and men, women and children from Bombay in vermilion and emerald. In the dark sanctuary, lighted by scores of torches, sit the white-vestured priests meditating on silence. There are people from Madras in fierce-colored purple robes with silver cloaks. Now and then they pour butter and sandalwood upon the fires. And, last of all, there are men from far-away Nepal and Thibet in blue and gray like their Himalayan dusk after a snowfall. These Thibetans cannot speak our language, so they say in Sanskrit: "We salute wisdom, we experience brother-hood today."

Outside mingle medicine men, gypsies with their dancing bears, snake charmers, and fakirs whom foreigners take for holy men. Then there are the real holy men, too, each of whom is holy in his own manner.

I saw the pilgrims coming out of the water. Their russet and green and orange draperies clung to them like so many liquid colors. And from the yellow sanctuaries and granite temples and red sandstone shrines came sounds other than human. From one came the cry of a trumpet, deeper than a bullfrog's croak. From another issued a rending sound of silk. From some came from shrill clash of cymbals or the clangor of gongs. And others, dripping with the drone of drums or the throbbing of stringed instruments, hushed the clamor of unrest in the pilgrim's heart and said to him as he marched from temple to temple, "All is peace. All is peace. Peace be unto all."

Apart from the great pageant of Kumbha-Mela I have a most personal reason for loving Allabahad, one which I want to impress deeply on our son's mind. Near the Nehru mansion, right across the road, is the temple of the sage, Bhardwaja. He was one of the great sages of the time of our ancient epics. It was at his door that Rama, the hero of the epic Ramayana, asked for hospitality.

It is said that Bhardwaja is the father of our Gotra family. The Mukhopadhayas, Anglicised to Mukerjis, are descended from the man who extended his meagre hospitality to Rama on this very spot. And Rama, you know, is considered an incarnation of God. Imagine, Rama Kamala lochana, He of the lotus eyes, was at our door asking for shelter; and we the poor Brahmins—we have been always poor—shared with him our leaf of lettuce, lotus buds, mangoes, and water from our spring—patram, puspam, phallam, toya! This need not make us proud, for there are innumerable families in India whose roots go deeper than ours. Many of them claim direct descent from the gods.

But to return to the story of Allahabad. Apart from being a famous place during the mythological times, it is very important historically. Buddha passed some days here. That is why there is a shrine, Stupa, to him near-by, in Bharhut. King Asoka erected an inscribed pillar here to commemorate the same sacred fact. Inside the fort, which was built by Akbar in the Sixteenth Century, at present occupied by the British troops, the Asokan pillar still stands. It also bears the inscription of Samudra Gupta about 300 A. D. and of Akbar's son in the Seventeenth Century.

Everything in Allahabad bristles with history. Besides, it is savage with beauty. Akbar's fort, where the Ganges bends like an arm to meet her sister Jumna, looks more like a fabulous work of art than a military structure. Its walls of red, now turning russet, though built of very thick slabs of stone, raise their soaring lines to the heavens as a warrior lifts his sword. The sculpture and the inscriptions, and mural decorations enchant one so that he can hardly imagine that here are housed aeroplane bombers, machine guns, poison gas tanks, and other monstrosities of the modern science of war.

Turning away from the river as we go into the city, its houses lacquered in vermilion, yellow, and blue, its temples, turrets and mosques, and last of all its peerless gardens planned in the Sixteenth Century, Khasroo Parks, where the very grass whispers of many memories of splendor, will ravish your senses and make your heart homesick for wonders that have passed. O Prayaga, thou Confluence of Gunga and Jumna, thy hands mingle the bitter beauty of memories with the most heartbreaking hopes. Indeed, thou art Allahabad—the Abode of God.

LETTER X

THE TWO NEHRUS

LETTER X

THE TWO NEHRUS

THE mind of the Western public is sometimes confused by the mention of several Nehrus. But the Nehrus who hold the attention of the Indian people are the seventy-year-old Pandit Motilal and his son, Jawaharlal. For the sake of definite designation we generally refer to them as Panditji, meaning the father, and Jawaharlal, the son. Though they differ greatly in taste and temperament, the two Nehrus share one thing in common: their dogged determination.

One time some forty years ago Motilal Nehru decided to modernize his entire family. Suddenly in his home, Purdah, seclusion of women came to be a thing of the past along with strict vegetarianism and priest-laden religious rituals. A very hot-tempered soul, he always practices what he says. A Brahmin himself, he told every other Brahmin who opposed his will to go on a planetary journey. In order to show that he was in right earnest, he filled his household with servants who observed no caste and ate meat. He is swift like the lightning when it comes to putting an idea into action.

Now I think you should be told what Panditji looks

like. First of all he has none of the sweetness of appearance that distinguishes his son. His square jaw, Roman
nose, thin, long lips, and tiger-like walk mark him out
to be a very haughty man. But the character of the
man really resides in his eyes. The large eyes though
they are blessed with long lashes have very little
shadow. They are fierce with light. Then, the right
eye differs in depth from the left. There are such lines
under the former as would indicate a telescope en-
dowed with ex-ray properties. One never enjoys the
glance of the Pandit's right searchlight. On the contrary the left one, equally well formed, is full of
sombreness and amity. My advice to you is that when
you meet Motilal gaze upon his left pupil; it will
make you most happy. I think his right eye makes him
the most brilliant lawyer and debater that he is; while
his left confers upon him a love of saints, artists, and
the peasantry.

It is no doubt that when he saw Gandhi the first
time, Panditji must have used his right eye, just to
make sure that the Mahatma was a saint. "Here is at
last a man who can defy all analysis and win the love
of all," Motilal must have exclaimed.

For Mahatma Gandhi is a man of "sky-scraping
humility." The effect of the meeting between the two
men can be measured by what followed. They became
fast friends. Motilal with his whole family embraced
Gandhism. He has made great financial sacrifices, suffered imprisonment, and offered his son and daughters

to the service of the nation without flinching. He has practiced non-violent resistance in the face of most serious provocations.

His sentence that I have already quoted gives you an idea that the old gentleman was no democrat. He loves distinction. And of all distinctions he values soul-excellence most highly. I should like to designate him a cosmological snob—the kind that is after spiritual nobility. And the same thing can be said against Jawaharlal, his only son. Rumor has it that the latter was "a great swell" one time. Harrow and Cambridge are the places where he went for his Western training. It is said that he was a friend of many royal aristocrats. His renunciation of the high world of society took place just after he had met Gandhi, a beggar in loincloth. Like his father he seems to have no resistance to spiritual nobility. Indians, both Hindus and Mohammedans, have succumbed to the charms of Gandhi. Barriers of religion have failed to hold people back as can be seen from the examples of such Mohammedans as Tyabji and Ansari, Nariman the Parsi, and Bajaj the Marwari multimillionaire. India is the only country in the world where the saint still wields the same power as he did in the Europe of the Middle Ages.

Now I hope you can slightly feel the feelings that drew the Nehrus, father and son, from the comfortable grooves of wealth and position to the via crucis of Gandhism. Both of them have endured imprisonment and other indignities at the hands of the British. Though they are inveterate enemies of the Empire they harbour no hatred against any Briton. Probably this latter fact makes them stronger than we can imagine. "For he who hates has already opened the gates of his home to his enemies."

Before leaving Allahabad I took down some of the remarks of Panditji that give us a glimpse of his mind.

I wanted to know from his own lips what he thought of the Hindu-Mohammedan unity. "As far as I can make out, dear Panditji, there is a widespread belief in America that there is no unity whatever between nearly eighty millions of Mohammedans and about two hundred million Hindus. What is your opinion?"

Motilal Nehru gave his opinion: "But we have unity. It is an accomplished fact between the youths of the two communities. In the All-India Youth League we have Hindus and Mohammedan boys standing shoulder to shoulder against the British. The place where we do suffer from some disunity is the relation of the old Hindus with the aged Muslims. My answer to that problem is that we should let death deal with the superannuated. After the cantankerous old chaps have died out we shall never hear of the Hindu-Mohammedan disunity. Thank God for the boys! They are no more interested in religious bigotry than I am. Yet the old men strut about on the dung-heap of dogmatism while Gandhism welds the young of India into one nationality."

"Panditji, what about the violence-loving revolu-
tionists?" I had to question him. "For the government
alleges that the conspirators are not only numerous,
but are really planning a violent revolution throughout the country." Motilal laughed. His has the most
youthful laughter that I have ever heard.

"What makes you laugh?" Earl was eager to learn
its reason.

"The British, I hope, are right," Panditji announced
most loudly: "I would welcome an India freed by
violence."

"Heavens!" I groaned in dismay.

Earl added: "I thought you were a believer in non-
violence."

"I am. Am I not practicing it? Have I not been
jailed for it? All the same I think those who practice
violence are not cowards. When the British go up and
bomb people from aeroplanes, nobody thinks of calling them dastardly assassins. Yet when some of my
countrymen plan a violent revolution we are pleased
to think of it in terms of shame. Well, I am no hypo-
crite. I will be grateful to any man who will free my
country.

"I am afraid the chances of such a thing are remote.
In the meantime we shall have to get along the best
we can with non-violence. And I for one shall stick
to Gandhism."

The last question that I put to him was: "You once
framed the Nehru Constitution for India. It was a

constitution on dominion basis. Why did you give it up?"

The old gentleman smiled ironically. "You have suspended your sense of humour for the time being, it seems. The Nehru Constitution, as it was called, though accepted by the All-Parties' Convention in India was spurned by the British. Even some of its severe critics admitted that my associates and I had hammered out a good basis for Indian Home Rule. Alas, it had one slight defect: the British spurned it. Well, you cannot get a status like that of Canada and Australia without the consent of the British. So I went in for independence to which their consent is not necessary. . . . Come, you have questioned me enough. Let me ask you—will you amuse me by visiting me occasionally when I am in jail? I shall be there soon enough. After my son, and Gandhi, it will be my turn to be the guest of King George."

"But, Panditji, why did they spurn the Nehru Constitution? Did they give any reason?" Earl persisted with his new question.

Panditji answered most courteously: "Our constitution was made before the Simon Commission. The British seem to hope that the Simon Report might be acceptable to India. This is the only reason I can think of. Of course you must not forget that our constitution demanded immediate dominion government. They would rather lose India than consent to that."

LETTER XI

A BRITISH POINT OF VIEW

LETTER XI

A BRITISH POINT OF VIEW

IN order to be fair I am inserting here some excerpts
from Lord Rothermere's article on India that appeared in the *Daily Mail* of May 16, 1930. It gives us
the beliefs of a great section of the British people
regarding England's relation to India:

" 'There is, I know, a school who say that we might wisely
walk out of India, and that the Indians would manage
their own affairs better than we can manage affairs for
them. Anybody who pictures to himself the anarchy, the
bloody chaos, that would follow from any such deplorable
step must shrink from that sinister decision.'

"These are not my words, profoundly though I believe
them to be the unalterable truth. They were uttered in the
House of Commons twenty-three years ago, by one of the
greatest democrats who ever sat there, in whose soul lived
a deep and instinctive hatred of all imperialistic exploitation, a man whose sympathy for his fellow human beings
of whatever race or colour was genuine and deep, besides
being far more accurately informed than are the sentimental delusions of many politicians in high places today.

"The speaker of these words of wisdom was that great
Liberal statesman, Honest John Morley, and they were inspired by all the knowledge and responsibility of his position as Secretary of State for India."

"A Democrat's Warning"

" 'Our Indian Empire would not be drifting into revolution, and the world towards a terrible Asiatic crisis, if men of the wisdom and calibre of Morley were in charge of that great Dependency today.'

"His clear vision of the facts of the Indian situation was not obscured by the complacent conviction, held by our Socialist Ministers, and their sloppy-minded auxiliaries on the front Conservative bench, that their own political sagacity has discovered the short cut to an Indian millennium. John Morley was content to carry on, worthily and patiently, the great duty he had inherited from generation after generation of the splendid British administrators who have been civilizing and serving that vast Oriental sub-Continent for 250 years.

"His practical mind was filled with facts, not vague sentimental prejudices. He saw plainly the danger of the policy of scuttle and abandonment in India which passes for high statesmanship with Socialist and semi-Socialist politicians on both sides of the House of Commons.

" 'How should we look in the face of the civilized world,' John Morley once asked a meeting of British electors, 'if we turned our back upon our duty and sovereign task? How should we bear the smarting stings of our own consciences when, as assuredly we should, we heard through the dark distances the roar and scream of confusion and carnage in India?' "

"I warn the men and women who read this article that their responsibility, as electors of Britain and therefore as rulers of India, is just as great and far more urgent today.

"The grim news that is continually reaching us from India, of British soldiers murdered, faithful Mohamme-

dan police clubbed to death or burnt alive, British women
and children huddled into forts or fleeing by train, the
great frontier fortress of Peshawar for days together in the
hands of Indian revolutionaries trying hard to lure the wild
tribes across the Afghan border into an invasion of the
frontier provinces, the law openly defied, the Union Jack
trampled under foot, the Viceroy's train bombed, stores
of smuggled weapons found and more arriving, and, in-
conspicuous but very serious, the warlike Sikhs, of whom
many regiments of the Indian Army are composed, resolv-
ing to support Gandhi's revolutionary movement—these
are not dramatic, unreal incidents in some picturesque
cinema film, but deadly threats to the lives and well-being
of British subjects, not only in India itself, but in Great
Britain also. We inherited an Empire so intact that we
took its continuance for granted. But if we prove unworthy
in the administration of what our fathers won and held,
our inheritance will fall in ruins about us.

"Why, then, are we deliberately sawing asunder the central geographic link in the world-wide chain of the British
Commonwealth of Nations?

"In a fresh proclamation issued earlier this week that
semi-Socialist, Lord Irwin, renewed the fatuous and im-
practicable pledge of Dominion Status for India which, encouraged by the connivance of his intimate personal friend,
Mr. Baldwin, he issued last November.

"The promise of Dominion Status should not be con-
firmed but cancelled. It takes two to keep a bargain. We
are released from ours by the open proclamation of the
intention of the Indian Nationalists to secede at the first
opportunity. Dominion Status would give them that opportunity. It means much more than did the "Self-government" vaguely held out in 1919 as an ultimate condition

for them by the late Mr. E. S. Montagu, the young Jewish banker who so disastrously obtained responsibility for our Indian affairs during the war.

"Since the Imperial Conference of 1926 Dominion Status confers not only the rights to maintain an army and have diplomatic relations with foreign countries. It is now admitted to imply full freedom to leave the Empire without let or hindrance, and that is exactly what the Indian Nationalist agitation is meant to bring about.

"The Montagu-Chelmsford scheme for Indianising the government of India was itself a concession to panic. These 'reforms' were rushed through Parliament in the hope of creating a favorable atmosphere for the Amritsar Congress of 1919.

"Our Indian Empire is still very much the greatest overseas consumer of British goods. Many authorities estimate that the proportion of the total trading, banking and shipping business of Britain directly dependent upon our connection with India is 20 per cent.

"Only since Nationalist influence was admitted to the Indian Administration have obstacles begun to be put in the way of our trade with the people of India. Before the war 60 per cent of India's imports came from Britain. Last year the proportion was only 43 per cent. Lancashire's cotton exports to India have fallen by one-half.

"The Indian Legislative Council has made it the law of the land that no Indian Government concessions shall be given to any firm whose capital is not in the native currency. The duty on our main export to that country— cotton piece-goods—has raised from 11 to 15 per cent. The Nationalist Party is pressing for the reservation of coastal traffic to vessels under Indian ownership and control, and for the full Indianisation of all public services."

"IF WE LEFT"

"It was British money and men that built up the steel industry in India, yet no bounties may be given under the Steel Protection Bill (though British money contributes to such subsidies) unless three-quarters of its directors are natives of India.

"British commercial interests in India are being deliberately strangled. Do electors at home yet realise that without our Indian trade it would be utterly impossible for the dole and pension services of Great Britain to be maintained?

"What the Indian agitators want is to force us to hand over India to the tyranny of a Hindu oligarchy, which would be the most jealously exclusive and the most shamelessly corrupt the world had ever seen. This would not bring peace to India—only oppression, extortion, civil war, slavery, famine, epidemics of disease, and, in the end, foreign invasion.

"We cannot turn our back upon our duty and compound with the open enemies of Britain. To do so would be such a cowardly betrayal of a great trust as would blacken our nation's name for ever.

"British rule in India is irreplaceable. Our duty there is not to argue with base agitators BUT TO GOVERN."

LETTER XII

OUR MODERATE AND LIBERAL POINT
OF VIEW

LETTER XII

OUR MODERATE AND LIBERAL POINT OF VIEW

THE Indian Moderate-Liberals are best represented by Sir Tej Bahadur Sapru, one of the ablest advocates and a real statesman of India. He has amassed a fabulous fortune by practicing law.

A Brahmin of an ancient lineage, he is not afraid of his wealth. For Brahmins are supposed to remain poor like the propertyless Guardians of Plato's Republic. His wealth sits lightly on him. Tej Bahadur is estimated as a gentleman of the British type rather than a Brahmin of the Platonic order.

He is very elegant to look at. Sportsmanlike in appearance, he carries himself with the jauntiness of a French cavalry officer. He is fair of complexion, like a Piedmontese nobleman. In fact his features are very Italian. The same graciousness and self-sufficiency that one sees in Italians of the old order characterize him. Besides he talks like an Italian. Takes great pleasure in using elegant Urdu. Prefers to say a thing in ten beautiful words where two ugly words would do. Though not a poet, his prose is as great as that of the

Urdu poet laureate, Sir Mohammad Ekbal. Tej
Bahadur's speech pours like honey into our ears.

Since he is the most important Moderate-Liberal, Mr.
Earl and I interviewed him in his baronial mansion.
There in chairs upholstered in exquisite morocco
leather, we waited hours before Sir Sapru appeared.
It was all very fitting. We, younger men, should learn
to await the arrival of our gifted and elegant elders.
At last when we beheld his entrance, like that of a
superb actor, we were thrilled at the finish of it. The
bow of that finely shaped head, the elegant sweep of
exquisite hands, the sumptuous salaam and the half-
veiled brown-gray eyes quietly studying our features—
indicated a very practical mind in the appearance of
a Brahmin. As he was seating himself in his divan,
helped by his attendant, I whispered into Earl's ears,
"I can see how the British succumb to his charms. But
we won't, shall we?"

Now that he was seated, Sir Tej began in English:
"The political situation is so changing that no forecast
is possible. So I shan't play the prophet, but a practical politician. . . . I think the Viceroy's call to a Round
Table Conference will lead to our attaining to Dominion Status, if all the Indian political parties could
be persuaded to go there with a united *front*. I am
initiating a conference of all the political parties except
the Congress of Gandhi in order to work out a treaty
on which we all can agree. Hindus, Mohammedans,
Parsis, Christians, and Pariahs—if they forge a united

opinion before starting for London, we shall be able to induce the British Parliament to accept it."

"But is there a united political opinion?" Mr. Earl wanted to know.

Sir Sapru: "Yes, and no. If you are thinking of the congress crowd of Mahatma Gandhi, then we are hopelessly divided. They are against any of us. There are no two opinions about Gandhi's sincerity and honesty, mind you. He is the greatest man living. But he is so unstatesmanlike in his opinions and action. He who holds the youth and the common people under his spiritual charm instead of giving them some counsel for moderation, is off on a campaign of law-breaking! He has literally divided the country into two halves. Until his inspiration has run its course, half of our population will remain intransigent.

"But nothing daunted I am organizing the other half. Hindus, Moslems, Pariahs and Christians of our school of thought are working out a series of proposals on which we are unanimous. We shall meet the representatives of Great Britain with them in order to bargain. We want the status of a dominion. For we do not think India can manage more than that at this stage of her evolution. We have plenty of well-trained Indians who can run a government shaped on the Canadian model."

"Canada is divided," I interrupted him, "into French Catholics, English-speaking Protestants; and Red Indian reservations just as we are between the Hindus,

the Mohammedans, and the Rajahs' Kingdoms. The
territory of the princes can be run like Ulster between
the British Crown and the Rajahs. Is that what you
mean?"

"A happy thought," explained Sir Sapru. "A constitution like that will cut the knot that binds us now."

"But what about the judicial system?" Mr. Earl
asked.

"That is easily arranged," remarked Tej Bahadur.
"It will be like your Federal system with this proviso:
namely, all cases can be appealed to the Privy Council
of Great Britain for, say four years. After that we shall
appeal to our own Supreme Court. Our Indian jus-
tices are fine men of great moral character. They are
equal to the best in the rest of the world. No, the Judi-
ciary offers me no stumbling block. It is the Gandhi
crowd who may succeed in poisoning the well of
England's good will toward us. Suppose outraged by
Gandhi's antics the British withdraw their offer of a
Round Table Conference. Would not that ruin India's
hope?"

Having gathered the crux of his political philosophy
from Sir Tej Bahadur Sapru, we took our leave.

You can see that he is a sincere statesman wishing
to serve the cause of his country within the frame of
British rule. He has represented India with credit at
the Imperial Conference. He can hold his own against
the best statesmen of Europe and America. Even if

you do not agree with him; it will not be fair to con-
demn him. After all, if India becomes free tomorrow,
we will have to ask him to serve in the cabinet with
the fierce Motilal Nehru. Of course Nehru probably
will be the Premier, and Sapru the Minister of Justice.
Do not sneer at Tej Bahadur.

LETTER XIII

A DANCER

LETTER XIII

A DANCER

ON our third morning in Allahabad, roused from sleep by the clamour of song-birds, I called out to my friend: "These winged chaps have no sense of design. They sing too much."

Mr. Earl answered: "What is ailing you?"

"The fact is that my mind is getting mouldy, listening to animadversions on India's current politics by too many great men. Let us spend this morning with the common people."

"I am game," agreed my friend. And forthwith plunged into his morning's meditation. Oh, these Americans, on time about everything!

I who had to wait during Mr. Earl's communion with the Infinite, put on my clothes, and took a walk in the immense garden of the Nehrus. It thrilled me to absorb India's odors and sounds. Champaks shed petals like soft gold on my head as I walked under their boughs. Bamboos whispered like a brook as the morning breeze shook the dew off their leaves.

A soft treading like that of barefoot boys drew near me. Behold, it was a caravan of camels caparisoned in tasselled red rugs coming down the tamarind-avenue.

Behind them screeched carts as they came laden with fantastic loads of jade and onyx. What were they? Loads of spinach, and pomegranate and red lentils. Suddenly in front of me leaped from the very ground an apparition of carmine: a street dancer dressed like the wonders of the Arabian nights. I begged her, "What seek you, O wonder of paradise?"

"I seek to please you with the witchery of my arms and feet. My drummer and lute-player are not far behind."

She took the trouble to show me her white teeth as she smiled consciously at me. "I am indeed charmed, O shamer of the moon," I answered. "But the fact is I have had no breakfast. I await an American still meditating on God. How can an empty belly relish the witchery of thy arms and feet? Come back an hour hence to enchant that alien who is at present communing with the Infinite."

The gypsy creature laughed out aloud, which gave her one more excuse to show her teeth. "It cannot be true," she opined that any hustling westerner can commune with God. "You surely mean it is your wife who is meditating."

It was my turn to laugh. "No wife of mine shall be permitted to meditate when I am feeling hungry, O upholder of witchery."

By now her drummer and lutanist having arrived, there was nothing for me to do but see the whole

performance through. It was not long before Earl
had come and joined me.

How can I describe the dancing? Only the excep-
tional dancers of Spain can use their hands and feet
as gracefully as this dancer of the United Provinces.
The bells on her ankle made silver whisperings as she
skipped on the grass and footed the measure of old
Mogul melodies. It took us back to the India when
the great Mogul built the Taj Mahal and bought each
dancer for his harem with her weight in rubies.

LETTER XIV

VISIT TO THE VILLAGERS OF THE UNITED PROVINCES

LETTER XIV

VISIT TO THE VILLAGERS OF THE UNITED PROVINCES

I HAD heard these many years that Jawaharlal was the idol of the Indian peasantry. So when he invited my friend and myself to visit some villages in his company, we were only too glad to accompany him.

There was a slightly funny event that took place at the inception of our trip. At the Allahabad railway station just as we had boarded the train, amid shouts of "Gandhiki Victory," from the assembled multitude, a terrific dust-storm rose choking everybody's mouth, ears, and eyes. Hard though we tried to cheer the President, every time we opened our mouths they were filled with the thick dust from the arid fields near by. Instead of ringing shouts of victory, Jawaharlal had to listen to the "vi-vi-vi-vi-gulp." It was pathetic. Luckily the air was so dark that not one of us could see the other one's plight at gulping down dust. Just then the train blew its whistle and we started. It is only too true that the President of India vanished in a cloud of dust.

Jawaharlal, his wife, Mr. Earl and I shut all the car

windows, turned on the electric lights, and then sat down to talk while the train steamed on. But there was no relief from the wind-blown dust. It burrowed its way through the double windows of the train and settled on every one and everything. Yellow, and black layer upon layer, stratum upon strata, the grains of dry soil covered our pores and skins. An intense irritation at every person, including our own selves, seized my being. I hated the universe and cursed the human race. Finding no relief in that, I said aloud, "I don't give a damn what happens to this country. Don't care who rules it."

Jawaharlal said sweetly, "That reminds me. Do you really want to serve your country? Or, are you here to look at it, mostly for amusement?"

"Well," I answered. "I want to serve it. But must it always be so dusty?"

"In your present state of health, you are no good here." He went on: "Go back to America and do what you have been doing. Write what pleases you."

Kamala, his wife, smiled and said soothingly, "Why don't you stay on? We will take care of you."

"No," I growled. "You do not want an invalid. You want to take care of India, not me."

Kamala now changed the subject and asked ironically, "Permit me to ask, what about some food, holy one?"

"The unholy one is not hungry, O voice of felicity," I returned.

She smiled and asked again: "Indeed, what can I do to remove the grains of irritation from your spirit?"

I answered her: "Recite some Sanskrit poetry, please."

But Jawaharlal interfered: "You know, I am a Shunyavadin—All-is-nothingist—but when Sanskrit is recited in my presence, I almost believe in the existence of the Deity."

"But how is it, an agnostic like you, pleases the Indian peasantry?" Mr. Earl wished to know. "*Au fond* they are the most religious people in the whole world."

In a few seconds the train stopped at a small station. We opened our car windows, fearing mortally the dust-storm. But instead of dust and wind, it seemed hundreds of peasants pressed their faces upon us, shouting, "Jawaharlal Nhruki Jai, Bharat Bhumiki Jai—Victory attends Jawaharlal, India wins victory."

Their cry sounded different. It issued not from their heads, as were the shouts of the members of the Youth League. Far from it. These peasants lifted their voices from the depth of their being. The bellow of their hungry bellies struck awe into our minds. It is not men and women, but the soul of India wailing. Indescribably tragic. May God preserve me from hearing such desolating voices the rest of my life!

They had come to see their chief and to receive instructions from him. Face upon hungry face, hollow eyes after hollow eyes, gazed and adored their chief. He spoke to them very gently; reverence cast its bloom

upon his speech. Here was Jawaharlal's real self
speaking.

Not to be outdone by his humility, their spokesman
said humbly, "Apto Karnadharji—you are the blessed
captain of our ship. What ever you wish shall be done.
Speak, O holy one, speak."

After the train had pulled out of that station, I asked
Jawaharlal, "How is it, that you, a Shunyavadin, who
considers that life ends with death, are called holy by
these people?"

The President answered with a smile: "It is truly
inexplicable. Ask my wife."

Now that the dust-storm was over, and the sky vestured in lavender and crowned with astarte stood
over the fields, where the dusk was stealing over the
spring harvest, we became quite still.

India has two harvest festivals; one in the autumn,
Dipavali, and the other in the spring, Rama Navami.
It is strange how the coming of spring is hemmed in
with rites in every country. Many Indians fast, practice
celibacy and pray for many weeks during the spring-
tide. In the province of Bengal the period is called Ga
jam and Chadak. Many young men and women put
on the ochre robe of the monk and practice numerous
penances. Then after a month and more, about mid-
April they change back to their usual mode of living.
What was it that started such traditions in each religion? The Christian Easter, Nebimusa and Ramadan

of other great creeds, why were they originated? Of course in an agricultural people like the Hindus, rituals are observed very strictly. I wonder what moral equivalent can we invent and enforce on highly industrialized cultures? After all, human nature is sensitive to seasons everywhere.

In India the springtime penances are more severe than anywhere else. This can be explained by the fact that in our climate, nature being full of extremes, human nature has to be severely disciplined. No wonder every spring season we go through some form of fasting and prayers.

While I was reflecting in the above manner, our fire-chariot had pulled into another station. Here too the same soul-shaking cries of hungry peasants greeted us. The same awe and love were showered on our young leader. And last of all gifts of fruits and flowers were showered not only on him but on the rest of us. "You too are great," I was told by their givers, "for you are associated with Jawaharlal—Bharat Bhumiki Jai—Victory to India!"

This last statement seemed to be the recurrent theme of every conversation of nearly two-thirds of the peasants. I cannot begin to tell you of the courage and hope that shone in the eyes of the villagers. It was a revelation to me. Jawaharlal has changed the moral tone of the rustics of northern India within the last ten years. No more cringing, evasive, tricky conspiracy of political agitators, but an open, honest, fearless statement of one's faith. Like David facing Goliath, the common people seem to stand facing the possibility of aerial bombers and machine guns. To win freedom may take years. But the stuff that make a people free is at last created. The peasants have lost their ancient fear. No matter where we traveled with young Jawaharlal, we perceived the beginning of a new world. India is reborn. Now she must advance.

LETTER XV

BENARES

LETTER XV

BENARES

OUR intimate studies of the country people were the most illuminating thing that Earl and I had done. But being a man of changeable temperament, one day I said to him, "Enough of India's independence. Let us go to Benares and look for holy men."

Kamala Nehru warned me, "There are no holy ones there. You will find Benares hollow and commercial. Come with us to other places and make a deep study of them."

"I cannot, O nightingale-tongue," I held out against her kindly pressure. "My nerves are done up. If I must perish, it shall be in Benares."

It was midnight when we were deposited at our monastery gate: no one there to greet us save divine Benares. The moonlit temples, the terraces, and the thick shadows that they cast enabled us to sense the psychic quality of the holy town in a most poignant manner. Lest it disturb our present experience, we stood still a long long time without making any noise. Again and again we heard, or, fancied that we heard:

"Brahma Satya, Jagat Mithya—only He is real, the world is unreal"—that eternal refrain of the mystics of India.

Don't knock on the gates. Listen to the silence of Benares. Far below us under the ramparts the Ganges turned and vanished into the wildernesses of India; above, almost touching our heads, the large tropical stars whispered: "This world is real to those the skin of whose minds is very green—Satyam jagat itivanam Samshrijayesyat Apakka chittyanam." Everything that you see and conceive is illusory. Even India's present servitude is a dream.

Slowly the monastery gates moved on their hinges, and from behind them approached three sleepy monks. They apologized for having gone to sleep. "For it is a poor host who does not stay up to welcome his incoming guest, no matter how late the latter might be." Alas, we were not interested in their noble apology. Our minds were still wrestling to cling to the psychic quality of Kashi, our holy city.

It was the next night that we had our most poetic experience of Kashi. At half-past ten we went out on a boat to see from afar its ghauts, temples, gardens, and palaces.

The city still hummed with noises. Sanskrit chantings in baritone, contralto singing of young street entertainers, occasional clangor of cymbals and gongs; then intense and harrowing shrill cries of the bereaved cremating their dead were drowned again and again under the fierce boom and thud of innumerable drums.

As the moonlight grew brighter, and the city receded farther, the ramparts of Benares rose firm and dark like gun metal. And on them rose black fortifications, and far-flung palaces dusty with moonlight. Forms which in daylight appear grotesquely glorious, of many conflicting colours and shapes, were wrought into a perfect design whose unity became impeccable and hard. The moon, riding high, "put all colours to sleep," revealing only the harmony of form.

Where form is completely realized there abides man's best experience of illusion. Benares is the only man-made place in India outside the Kailasa Temple of Ellura that compels us to admit the formlessness of the universe through a completely wrought-out sense of form.

LETTER XVI

A HOLY MAN

LETTER XVI

A HOLY MAN

BEFORE our reaching Benares, we were informed by more than one person of intelligence that there are no more authentic holy men there. "Many spiritual men have followed Gandhi's example and entered politics. And if there be any one left, they must have gone away far from Kashi."

I was not discouraged by such people. But when in the monastery many an ochre-robed young monk told me that there was no very important holy man in the city, I was made unhappy. Still I persisted in my search. Even common fakirs and rascals I interviewed, hoping to find among them a Son of God. Alas, we found none. Mr. Earl, utterly convinced by now, told me one day, "There is none to be found here. But then it does not matter. The man we are looking for is in Behur, not far from Calcutta. Why not enjoy the city itself here? Do not wear yourself out looking for a master. By the way, what about that Pali scholar we met the other day?"

"I am not fond of those inspectors of the mental morgue, the scholars, in Benares, my friend." I went

on, "either there is a holy man whom I am to meet
in Benares, or, my name is mud."

Earl retorted, "We have been wallowing in mud for
days, it seems. And shall for weeks."

Alas, he spoke too soon. That very afternoon at sundown the miracle took place. According to the Hindu
Punjika, Almanac, it was a propitious day. In my case
it turned out to be profoundly so.

We had just come from the bazars buying incense.
The sun had set and the twilight "like a pigeon's
throat" was gleaming in the sky and the streets. Rose
roofs of the houses, their violet walls were drenched
in a subtle tone of iridescence. Earl and I were passing
by a dingy lane. There an ordinary sight greeted us.
A very virile middle-aged man, robed in ochre, was
opening a door. There was that something about him
which compelled attention. My friend whispered, "I
seem to know him."

"So do I," I exclaimed in turn.

Now having opened the door the man straightened
himself and looked at us. It made us stand still and
gaze at him quietly.

"Welcome," the man said. "You have come on an
auspicious evening." Then he broke out into English.
"Mr. Earl, what a tie between you and me!"

By drawing close, we succeeded in recognizing him.
He was old Kalirishi of Benares. Imagine a man about
seventy years old at 1920 now grown young enough to
look forty. Is it any fault of ours that we had failed

to identify him? Alas, he refused to talk to us at length
on that occasion. He smiled at me and remarked,
"Your mind is itching for scenes of action to study. It
is not quiet enough to pay attention to anything else.
That which makes your thoughts alight on their objects is not dying to hear words of wisdom. Am I
right?"

"How do you know, my lord?" Earl sought for
more light on the subject.

Kalirishi grinned, then added: "It is not you that I
am reproaching, but my countryman, Dhan Gopal. He
has the journalist's unwholesome love of knowing
events; as if events were not the results of ideas. Now,
go about the neighborhood of Benares for awhile,
studying the political unrest. After that is finished
with, when you are completely still in mind and spirit,
come to me. I shall fill your hearing with my words."

LETTER XVII

INTRANSIGENT PEASANTS

LETTER XVII

INTRANSIGENT PEASANTS

THE very next morning I set out to study the mentality and the organization of the intransigent peasants of the neighboring villages. The same state of unrest as we had observed elsewhere pervaded the spirit of more than half the people. One reason for the present psychology of the peasantry in the United Provinces is plain. The largest part of the Provinces is owned by zemindars, rich landlords. The largest bulk of the cultivators are tenants. Unlike the province of the Punjab, the United Provinces have very few peasant proprietors. Being nothing but perpetual toilers on land which they do not own, the rural population, almost all of the Gangetic Valley, suffer from an inordinate amount of land-hunger. Since most of the zemindars are not ideal landlords, they have permitted innumerable grievances, both real and imaginary, to accumulate in the hearts of their ryots, tenants. Given the existence of such a state of affairs, the appeal of Gandhimen: that "when India is free we shall have a more equitable distribution of land," cannot but penetrate the soul of the "Krishan, harvest-creators." The latter in many villages have interpreted "equitable dis-

tribution of land" in a most generous fashion. More
than one young peasant hopes to expropriate the
zemindars when "freedom's battle is won." What fools
we can be! When I informed them that it would be
far easier for them to annex the moon they considered
me nothing but a dilettante. "Meditate upon my
words," I exhorted some of the peasants. "If the
British go, the new state will need money. It will have
to come to terms with the rich landlords who alone
can lend it the money to get started. Not that you
will not get some of your big grievances removed, but
it is sheer self-delusion on your part if you think you
will achieve peasant-proprietorship in your province.
Don't expect too much of any state. States are children of compromise: they will fulfil our minor hopes
by defeating our major expectations. Besides no one
can be sure that the coming revolution will take
place."

Within a day or two I had the opportunity to meet
many leaders of the peasantry in a secret conclave in
Benares. They were meeting to decide on not paying
a minor impost, "the chowkidari or watchmen's tax,
besides ordering every community to make salt."

The meeting took place in a rich man's house. And
my presence there, though not according to the rules,
was permitted on grounds that would become clear
later. Because I promised it, I have to conceal the men's
names; and must speak of their work without describing the faces of most of them. Yet the resolutions that

they passed were nothing very serious. I have already mentioned their decision to break the Salt Law on the morrow.

The next item they voted upon was a complete boycott of British goods of every description. Up till now they had boycotted only cotton goods. But from now on the boycott should be extended to anything made in Great Britain. Last of all, in a casual manner, they ordered every community not to pay the watchmen's tax.

Then they talked and deliberated on the exact time for suspending payment of all taxes. Here I invite you to exercise your imagination. Picture to yourself a long room with red walls, and seated on its grey floor about sixty peasants, two doctors, and three lawyers. Owing to their being dressed in Khaddar, Gandhi homespun, from top to toe, you could not tell the caste and religion of any two persons present. The only thing you could tell was their ages. More than half of them were men past forty.

After the programme of the main meeting had been concluded, the reason for my presence there was explained. I was described as a newspaperman of "unimpeachable veracity" from the United States. Everybody present had a hard time keeping a straight face. In order to make them trust me, I said, "I need not be introduced as a press agent in order to learn how you work. I am not a representative of the house of printing. I am a humble lover of my race."

"Bahoot Accha, most excellent!" exclaimed a number of them. Feeling that they were on the verge of putting their faith in me, I requested: "O assembled civilized beings, it is an open secret that you are planning to go on tax-strike. May I ask are you prepared not to pay any tax next July to the Myrmidons of the State?"

A spell of real silence fell upon them. Peasants the world over are suspicious and reticent. Seeing that they would not say anything, and the time at my disposal being brief, I begged them anew. "If you do not pay taxes the British will auction your houses, and cattle. It is fortunate that most of you of the Gangetic valley are tenants. Were you owners of your fields instead, the government would confiscate your lands as well. Another thing, the State may jail you without bringing any of you to trial. Have you visualized all the consequences? Can you still think of offering civil disobedience?"

As if I had put thorns into every man's flesh, most of them winced. Then a very deluge of remarks came from their hitherto reticent tongues.

A man almost the color of shining copper in gray homespun spoke very loudly to the rest: "Let us tell the truth to this America-returned man without mendacity. The C. I. D. knows all that we are preparing to do. For the secret police learns of our most important decisions just after we have made them. Allah knows that we are planning a revolution that will alter the heart-beat of the State. Let us give this bazar-writer of America the information he seeks. Why withhold it from an ordinary story-teller?"

"As you wish, Sheikhji." His friends consented; and let him speak.

Sheikhji thrust forward his long Mohammedan nose as a gesture of defiance. He stroked his beard with trembling long fingers. As a man unaccustomed to talking, he pitched his voice too high. It was deafening. But what he lacked in art was erased by his sincerity. "Allah has given us no smooth living," he proclaimed. "One time we are ruined by inundation, another time by famine. If some year there is a good crop, the landlords and the money-lenders take possession of more than half. Now you say that if we embark upon a tax-strike we will be ruined. Sach bāt—the true speech betrays the fact that we have known ruin and hunger as our right and left hands. You, O story-teller from Markin—Mooluk, America, are using words only. It is we who know their meaning. The government can do no worse than a famine does. The landlords cannot do more harm than the rivers in flood. He who sleeps on the rock of calamity need not be afraid to be roused by an earthquake."

The speaker was now greeted thus: "Keyabat, Sach bachan, Tamam—what word can describe his eloquence, true word, and 'enough spoken.'"

Seeing that they were communicative now, I probed their minds further: "Will you keep your pledge of complete non-violence that you have given Nehru and Gandhi?"

Sheikhji's long narrow eyes flashed with anger. They "blossomed into flowers of burning passion." "We have to, the Almighty knows. In a country where it is considered a crime to carry a steel blade more than a foot long, what else is there to do but the practice of non-violence? I am a Moslem. Allah Karim, am not a Hindu vegetarian like Gandhi. I would fight with arms if I could. But can my fist silence guns? I am driven by necessity to be non-violent like the Hindus. Let us try to go on a strike in the matter of paying taxes. Who knows Kismet may compel victory for our race."

Later on when I reported the reason given for complete non-violence by this farmer to Earl, he was not pleased. He asked fretfully, "Why is it that these people do not care to practice non-violent resistance as a nobler form of conduct? They always mention very materialistic grounds on which they have chosen Gandhism."

"That's the worst of all orientals!" I went on lamenting: "We never do a noble thing without giving an ignoble reason for it. We are so practical. The curse of India is pragmatism. It is awful."

But to return to Sheikji and his friends; instead of answering any further questions put by myself, they urged me to make a heartening speech to them. It was the most nervous task that I have ever done.

Just imagine me trying to inspire not Americans, but matter-of-fact Hindus and Mohammedans. Because there was no alternative, I settled down to hearten them.

"O assembled civilized ones, forgive my poor Hindustani. My mouth has spoken an alien tongue too long. My throat sings foreign words habitually. Oh, how to kindle my mouth with the flame of Hindustani! May your presence smite my mind so that it will act like whetted steel. And my million Kasoors, mistakes, your tortured patience must forgive."

"Enough of thy exordium, speak truth," a young peasant interrupted me.

But refusing to be punctured by his impatience, I continued: "I saw India and the Gandhi movement of eight years ago. Then we were great though ultimately beaten by the British. I remember how Gandhi and more than thirty thousand others were jailed. But out of that defeat our country garnered a single harvest of victory: namely, the whole race obeyed its saint-leader and remained strictly non-violent. Three hundred million people behaved as Gandhi had enjoined them. A moral triumph of such magnitude was unheard of. During those days there was no doubt of India's spiritual primacy over all mankind.

"Today a different spectacle greets my eyes. Though all of you will keep your promise of non-violent resistance; though our people will not think of harming an English woman or an English child; though

you are heart and soul for independence through boycott of British goods and non-payment of taxes; yet I
perceive grave disillusionment in all. You are abolish-
ing caste among the Hindus, not because caste is bad;
but because you want to unite yourselves completely
to fight the British. All the Hindu and Mohammedan
volunteers, mostly men and women, eat together and
work together; not that they have started practicing
brotherhood, but because by eliminating creedal differ-
ences they think they can fight the foreigner most
successfully. Among yourselves here men and women
are working in the open; not because you want to
free your women. On the contrary you do it; for free
women mean more soldiers who will strive with you
against your alien rulers. You want women's freedom
for the sake of welding the many members of your
race into one fighting unit.

"It is true you are no more afraid of the British. I
concede that the old cringing cowardice of my boy-
hood is gone from the land. Gandhi has healed us of
fear. But it will be much the same state of sickness if
we disease ourselves with hatred of the foreigners who
rule our country. Hate is no better substitute for fear.
I admit that the new movement is ironing out disunity
between castes, communities, and sexes. But these revolutionary changes may ruin us if they are the offspring
of our hate. Beware! Hatred, O civilized beings, is more
sinister than the old disease of fear.

"Having admitted our common weakness let us for

a moment examine our real strength. Our strength lies not in disillusion but in our old illusion: Ahimsa, non-hate. What makes our conquered, humiliated, and grossly libeled India the foremost country of the East and second to none in the West is non-hate. We have never hated anyone.

"Now hate is within our gates. The population of the large cities and factories that I have recently studied are saturated with it. The mill hands of Bombay and other places are the greatest haters of the world. Their hatred is rooted in their grievances against their soulless employers and the British military police.

"You, who are seventy per cent of India's sons, are not so tainted. The tillers of our soil are pure. You can win without stooping to any kind of hate. You will win if you resist without 'Himsa.' Do not betray Gandhiji, your leader. Through him we have earned our prominent position among the nations of the world. Be true to his creed of non-hate, and you will make India the most exemplary country on earth. I beg you, brothers, to work with hateless hearts. Hold on to our ancient ideal of Viswa—maitri, world-amity and non-hate."

How do you think they received my eloquence? The young peasants greeted it with contempt. While the old fellows applauded me heartily.

No sooner had I finished than the youthful peasant,

who had tried to interrupt me before, rose to his feet and made a speech in a most rasping style. He had the look of an artist, in fact effeminate and closely resembling some portraits of that mad poet Shelley. He must have come from a highly inbred chattri, princely, tribe. All I can recall of his turgid oratory is this paragraph: "When all three non-violent weapons fail, we will have to fight with weapons of violence. Our first weapon is already useless. Though hundreds of us have broken the salt-monopoly of the State we have not succeeded in making salt cheaper, nor the salt-tax a thing of the past." . . .

"But surely your second weapon has not failed," I heckled him. "The boycott of foreign cotton goods is progressing well!"

Nothing daunted this Indian village Hampden hit back: "It will fail if our third weapon fails to bring us success. Boycotting British goods even if it is successful, will be of no value unless it is backed by our non-payment of taxes. How do you know our third weapon will win, O journalist from America? Remember we have been beaten before. We may be beaten again. . . . Then we will have to organize a violent revolution."

Of course I did not want him to go unchallenged. So I rose to my feet once more and said briefly: "If non-violence fails now, my answer is that you must plan and organize a more scientific non-violent revolt. It is my firm conviction that its failure will not dis-

credit non-violent revolutions, but will go to show
that you have not worked out its most significant scientific details. You must win through a better-planned
non-violence."

That is as far as I went that day. I am still wondering if Gandhism will be tried once more in case the
present revolution is successfully suppressed. It is no
use hiding the fact that the revolting youth of the
country may be so disillusioned that they will go right
into organizing a violent revolution when they come
out of their jails. That will slowly push India into
such a chaos that it will be ten times worse than what
has overtaken China.

But here you may ask for some further reason for
so much sympathy for civil disobedience among the
peasants of northern India. Their second reason is all
unreason: it is their love of Jawaharlal Nehru whom
they call Adarsha Brahman, ideal Brahman. You cannot grasp its true significance if you are not born a
Hindu. We apply that phrase to a Brahmin who has
never eaten meat, never drunk alcohol, never crossed
the ocean, never gets angry, never hates, never fights
an enemy, and never owns wealth. There is only one
of those injunctions that Jawaharlal has lived up to.
He never hates. Outside that, he has crossed the ocean,
for he is a Cambridge graduate. He fights like a lion.
He is considered dangerous enough to be jailed by
the British more than once. I have known him to lose
his temper and curse everybody in Latin and Sanskrit.

The latter curses generally come true, for they are done in Deva vesa. So I do not see any objective date on which the people base their conclusion that Jawaharlal is an Adarsha Brahman of the orthodox mould. I think that no matter how many objective reasons you dig up to show that they account for the rebellious mentality of our people you shall not reach the root cause of the present unrest. To my mind the source of our trouble lies in our thinking. Somehow we have come to think that it is a disgrace to be ruled by foreigners. Given this thought it is very easy to discover objective grievances for its basis.

We are a deeply subjective race. He alone knows us who has made a study of our minds. How mind-bound we are you can gather from a few words that every mother teaches her child from its cradle onwards: "Mano eva Jagat Sarvam—All that is, or seems, comes from your mind." Gandhi, Nehru and others may be utterly impractical, but the people's thought tells them that they will lead them to victory. So they try to follow such leaders. Whenever you are dealing with an average un-Westernized Hindu, deal with his thoughts that are behind his words. My mother used to say, "Listen to your neighbor's silence, not to his words." The trouble with the Viceroy and all the British is that they are using too many words. If they could listen quietly to the silence of our masses they would better understand what was in the mind of India.

LETTER XVIII

BREAKERS OF THE SALT LAW

LETTER XVIII

BREAKERS OF THE SALT LAW

PROBABLY you want to know how the Gandhi-men go about breaking the State law against manufacturing and selling salt. Though the law is broken in a different manner in every province, the forces of the government seem to exercise one universal technique regarding suppressing it.

I think I shall stage this common occurrence in holy Benares for you to see. It is the loveliest spot in India; and besides in this neighborhood the suppression of the salt-breakers was done solely by bludgeoning. So far as I know there has not been any gun-play hereabouts. And I think you can endure a sight of human suffering in which neither rifle-fire, nor bombing has had a part. I will do my best to keep the events that you are about to behold within the limits of your endurance. Trust me to do the staging decently.

Imagine yourself sitting on the balcony of a house about sundown a few days ago.

All the colours of space were there: the houses and their history, the terraces thronging with people, and the main road below lined with red-turbaned policemen bearing lathis, staves five feet long and about one inch in diameter. . . .

I am sorely tempted to describe the colours of the sunset that stung one's eyes. But I must resist. Just think of yourself looking down on a dusty road white with chalk, bristling with cruel possibilities. There is no one there except two rows of policemen.

Everybody was tense, specially the women pilgrims. They muttered repeatedly "Kidarsay Iyega—which way are they coming?" No one knew, not even the police. Every moment conjecture rose upon conjecture making the place throb with expectancy.

Now suddenly through a narrow serpent-shaped alley emerged a procession of about fifty boys, many of whom wore handcuffs on both hands, chanting— "Victory! Victory to Gandhi!"

This surprised everybody. The policemen too were surprised, as they gazed upon the procession led by handcuffed youths robed in white, like bulls going to the sacrifice.

"Why have they allowed their hands to be tied up this way?" asked Mr. Earl.

I explained: "It is a part of the Gandhi creed. Some of them have taken this measure against themselves so that in case the policemen bludgeon them, the nationalists, even if they want to, shall not be able to hit back. Look. . . ." As if by magic from every direction came buyers of contraband salt. They took from each one of the volunteers his two handfuls of salt, then thrust money into them. Those wretches tightly closed their fists once again in order to keep the cash.

Now suddenly the Police Captain gave his orders; that instant the Myrmidons of the law thrust themselves forward. At first, they roughly elbowed numerous salt buyers. But that did no good. So they were forced to take their second measure, not only prearranged but already rehearsed many times, it seemed.

They thrust the ends of their staves into the small of each person's back. One, two, three . . . the salt-buyers began to give way. Some of them disappeared into alleys and doorways.

At last there remained a small crowd of buyers who could not be prodded out of the street. No doubt they were gifted with some determination. The police force went on ramming into them. At this stage another incident came into evidence. Instead of enduring the staves passively some of the people endeavoured to deprive their assailants of their weapons by snatching the "lathis" from the hands of the police. In fact one of the lictors of the law was thus ignominiously disarmed. This made matters worse. Now inspired by some kind of fear, the policemen started to beat up everybody in sight.

Instantly the salt-buyers were put to flight. This seemed to amuse all the spectators. The more the

beaten men ran away the better grew the fun. Here
was the psychological moment to call a halt. . . . Had
the police done so it would have pleased all and sundry.

But the forces of the law were so wrought up that
they set to belabour the volunteers whose hands, you
will recall, were tied up. All of them, refusing to run
away, had to be beaten 'til a majority was felled to
the ground.

The present event of the drama instead of amusing
them made the spectators rage. They began to scream:
"The police are sons of pigs. May God feed them
sticks. Hell was their cradle and hell shall be their
grave. Down with the sons of dogs. Down with the
sons of asses."

The shouts and screams of the enraged observers
had the effect of bringing the wielders of the clubs to
their senses. Their chief blew a whistle, and gave the
order for Greftar: "Arrest the rest!"

This was easily done, for none offered any resistance.
At this point the mob set up a fiercer noise of curses
and threats: "Unturban the red-turbaned swine; take
their staves from them, and ram them down their
gullets. O the dogs, the soulless dogs!"

Unable to endure the sight before them any longer,
the bravest among them commenced to come down
on the police from the rear amid most deafening
shouts.

However, they could not get anywhere near the
clubbing constables. For, lo, with a sudden clangor of

horn, wheels, and bells about three police lorries drove
in from the right and stopped dead. Out of them leaped
about a score more guardians of the peace. They aided
their friends in rounding up their prisoners. Before
we could count how many, the captives had been lifted
into the vans and driven out of sight. Thus having
stunned the gaping mob with this last touch of drama,
the entire police force had vanished into the augment-
ing gloom of the night.

Now that the barricade of motor vans had been
removed, all of the people dashed forward to succour
the conscious, the semi-conscious, and the unconscious
Gandhimen littering the street. It was very easy to give
help to men whose hands were not tied up. But the
trouble became most annoying with the handcuff-
wearing youths. For the fellow who is supposed to
unlock the men's handcuffs was swept away from his
comrades by the vociferous crowd. Fortunately the
people being amenable to reason made way for him
to resume his task of freeing his friends.

It took him ages to free each volunteer groaning
on the ground, because he had to work in the dark.
O Lord, the time these Orientals can take!

At last the Red Cross of the Congress Party appeared
on the scene with stretchers and cars. Of course since
it was India the crowd that sought to show sympathy
got in the way of the doctors and the First Aid Crew.
Thank God for our capacity for enduring pain! Those
battered and bleeding volunteers made light of their

aches and wounds while they waited patiently to be bandaged and taken home. One of them said jocularly: "Thanks to my tied-up hands; otherwise I would have lost the ten rupee note for which I sold my portion of salt. Since I could not use my hands for fighting I held on to the cash with both fists. There is sense in this handcuffing: you may save money by it. And God knows the movement needs cash badly."

"Where does all this money go?" we asked.

He smiled while they lifted him on a stretcher. "Hai," he called, "treasurer, where art thou? Here be thy ten rupees."

The money fell on the street from his blood smeared hands. "Now," he urged the two stretcher-bearers, "home, on my cart."

The mob followed the stretchers shouting, "Victory!"

Hardly had they gone out of sight, when far off boomed the gongs of Viswanath's temple, announcing the hour of Arati, evening silence. From the temple of the lord of the universe bellowed hundreds of drums like "bulls at pasture." With the last wounded volunteer the crowd moved away from the street. The city lights had been turned on by now. Under one of them we saw a mammoth white cow looking down her nose in the attitude of uttermost contempt.

The voice of a pilgrim from behind us chanted, "Satya meva jayete nanritam—not untruth, but Truth alone triumphs at the end. Maunam Chaivasmi goohyanam—I am God, the supreme secret; for I am Silence."

It may sound like an anticlimax but I must tell you what happened next. I looked at a white temple to my right up whose steep side my gaze travelled till it reached the very top where sat an enormous monkey, more fearful in appearance than all the gargoyles of a gothic cathedral. Hewn out of jet, mantled with stars, that beast seemed to grin contentedly at the folly of man. What malice had prompted him to his royal seat there in order to see the afternoon's fight? Why was he still there? To point what moral?

LETTER XIX

AS A BEGGAR SEES IT

LETTER XIX

AS A BEGGAR SEES IT

IN order to get a beggar's point of view on the Indian unrest the next morning I led Mr. Earl to that part of the city where pseudo-spiritual men and women, fakirs and beggars, keep shop. These, no Hindu knows how, foreigners enjoy calling our representative holy men.

After interviewing some fakirs we reached the booth of an old sitter-on-nails [1] whom I knew. I loved the shaggy and dusty old fellow who spent two hours a day on his bed of nails and made his living out of it. After all, he was a good magician. He who could sit on nails in order to avoid working at a decent trade is no ordinary fraud. There must be a touch of talent about him.

Seeing me approach, the ancient rascal opened his eyes wider and wider. "Hello, the gods be praised," he exclaimed. "Here you come again with another American. Good. The gods are benignant. How much can your friend pay if instead of sitting I lie on my face and stomach on these nails?"

"He will not pay a penny, O dispenser of enchant-

[1] See "Visit India With Me."

183

ment, Taj jabwala," I warned him. "My friend has been here before. He knows Benares better than some of us. Besides he is a scholar and an artist. He cannot pay."

"But this is a strange species of American!" He was astonished. "American without gold to throw away? What calamity has harmed your race?"

Mr. Earl smiled with malice and made this enlightening remark: "The stock market has touched bottom, my friend. Besides, I feel so much at home in Benares, like your fellow-citizens I am not interested in magic. But I will pay you half a dollar if you give us information."

"Indeed the Americans are impoverished. What in the name of Heaven is a stock market?"

I told him that it is a place where "Dalals, the brokers, take money out of one set of pockets and stick it into another."

Earl embellished it further. "It is the prison of the American Soul. It is sometimes called Wall Street."

The nail-sitter spat three times across the street into the gutter. Then getting down from his perch he squatted on the roadside. "Now that I have spat on your stock market three times it cannot harm me. If you spit at any invisible evil three times it dies instantly. Having made myself safe from the market, I shall give you all the information in the universe for half a dollar. But not a penny less." He bargained obstinately.

Mr. Earl handed him his due then asked, "What is your interpretation of yesterday's bludgeoning of the salt-vendors?"

Suddenly the nail-sitter burst out laughing. Mr. Earl and I were dismayed. We waited patiently for our entertainer's return to reason.

After having laughed his fill he apologized: "I never expected a question like the one you asked. I thought you wanted to learn the entire secret of nail-sitting. I never dreamt that . . . ho, ho, ho."

I commanded him sternly to answer my friend's question. "Do you not see, O heaven-splitting laughter, you are drawing idle passersby in large numbers with your mirth?"

"I shall desist laughing." Then collecting himself he asked, "Why did you choose me to answer such a question?"   ,

"That is my fault," my friend admitted. "I saw you here five years ago plying your trade, deceiving my fellow-countrymen with the idea that you were hundred per cent holy. That convinced me that you know the weaknesses of mortals whether they are of the East or the West.

"Now this Gandhi business that is sweeping the country has bewildered me. You who know the secrets of human nature, since you exploit it so well, may enlighten us."

Flattered to the zenith of his conceit the poor beggar set out to enlighten us with the eagerness of an infant. "That bludgeoning of last night is nothing so astounding as what I saw a few weeks ago during Kumbha festivals both here and Prayaga, Allahabad. All Benares was startled to its belly-pit when the high-priest of Hinduism, Pandit Malavya, blessed over twenty thousand Pariahs, saying, 'You are untouchables no more. Now all the religious privileges of the other castes you should claim as your birthright. So be it, so be it, so be it, he repeated. All the witnesses, numbering about fifty thousand, reiterated the last three words after him. Then the casteless ones performed their ablutions in the Ganges, put on radiant raiments, and entered places of worship where no Pariahs had set foot before. Of course those people made generous offerings to everybody. That day I earned thirty-five rupees, fifteen dollars. Now I am for the restitution of all rights to the Pariahs. They are more generous than the American tourists. The priests of the different shrines will tell you the same truth. That day the priestly gang coined money. That is why we want droves of Pariahs here once a month to be blessed out of their castelessness by Malavyaji."

Mr. Earl said to me in a language that the nail-sitter did not know a word of, "As the other castes grow apathetic to religion the underdog is being placated by privileges in order to keep the priests alive. So it is economics that will wipe out the status of the untouchables in a dozen years. The Lord fulfils himself in devious ways."

"What happened in Prayaga in Kumbha-Mela time last month?" I asked the fakir.

"Oho, that, that will surprise you the most. There in Allahabad had assembled ten million people to acquire merit by bathing in the Tribeni. No restriction was permitted against the Pariahs. I made good money there the two days I was visiting. Do you know this: that over a million people took inoculation against cholera from Europe-returned Indian doctors. I speak God's truth: these eyes beheld meat-eaters inoculating Brahmins and Pariahs side by side. That ought to make your jaw turn into pulp."

"Not yet," I remarked. "I foresaw and predicted all that in "My Brother's Face." Have you read it?"

My words made the magician angry: "I am no fool. I never read books. I study people as they pass where I sit."

Mr. Earl pressed him further: "How do you interpret all the contests between the Gandhimen and the police?"

"The thing will bring dishonour to the state," he opined crisply. "I know the way human beings take these Gandhi tricks."

"Tricks!" exclaimed Mr. Earl and I with horror. "The very idea!"

"Ho, ho, ho," laughed the nail-sitter. "You have no sense of humour in your bowels. Do you not see how carefully those volunteers plan the bludgeoning? They see to it that they have a vast concourse of spectators.

They have their own hands tied in order to rouse their countrymen's pity. Then they invite to be belabored by the state with huge sticks. Why, no theatre can produce a more pity-rousing piece. It is full of tricks. The spectators all fall for it. They become so roused that they like to throw the British into the gutters. No, it is bad for the state. If I were the sircar, the police, I would let the fools sell their salt, but would put them out of business by selling state-made salt ten times cheaper. Why wield the bludgeon?"

"Now, look here," I asked, "O thou blade of insight, if caste goes, religious bigotry goes, and the seclusion of woman goes, would not these strengthen people to win freedom from the British?"

"No," he growled like a tiger.

"Why not?" Earl demanded.

"Because," answered our friend, "most of the people of our country lack tenacity. All that mob that howled for Gandhi's victory as they went home last night will have forgotten their own voices the next week. Look, O giver of half-dollar, have I not talked enough for that piece of money? Now I shall go back to my real trade. Watch me sit down on those nails with the ease of a caterpillar amid leaves. Farewell. I have done with talking politics."

"You know," I spoke very nicely, "you speak of your own countrymen as does the *London Daily Mail*."

"What is his status?" asked the fakir. Apparently he had assumed the paper to be a person.

"It is an instrument of speech employed by millions of British men and women," I informed him.

"But don't the British eat meat?" he asked out of a clear sky.

"Of course they do, you know that, O fox of intelligence," I flattered him.

"If they eat meat I do not agree with them," he declared flatly. "Meat-eating is sinful."

He declined to speak any more on politics. So we left the nail-sitter to whom meat-eating is the Nadir of sin.

LETTER XX

AS A HOLY MAN SEES IT

LETTER XX

AS A HOLY MAN SEES IT

MR. EARL and I had enough of politics. In any case what we had seen and heard of recent events in India had confused our minds. Instead of more clarity more stupefaction seemed to come over both of us. There was no other way of finding ourselves save by going to a holy man. And had not the holy man we had found told us to come back to him?

That our friend Kalirishi is the last holy man of Benares, those who know the authentic article will concede. After him will begin the reign of the pseudo-holy, and the frauds so dearly cherished by Western tourists. Benares like the rest of India will go through a great transformation.

It was imperative that we should call upon him in order to apprehend the inwardness of the revolutionary changes happening in Hindustan. If there was anyone who could show us the Rupam Kalyana tama, the most radiant face of the sun behind the black cloud of calamity, it was Kalirishi. He had the power to pierce through the present gloom.

So from the nail-sitter's place we walked straight to him through the dusty lanes and between ancient mansions from whose roofs cynical monkeys gazed at us with the contempt of disillusioned deities. After glancing at them once or twice, Mr. Earl remarked: "Only a naive mind could infer that this, our innocent human race, was born of those sophisticated baboons."

Soon we found ourselves at Kalirishi's place. The master was meditating. We had to wait for over an hour before he would consent to come out of the silence. Fortunately his cell was cool, and the dusty road outside, forbidding with heat, turned the calamity of waiting an hour into the blessing of enjoying the cool.

Have you ever seen a man give out light through every pore of his body? Such was Kalirishi when he came out of his meditation. He gazed at us not from his eyes, but from an immense distance behind his eyes.

After blessing us he sat down between Earl and me. Slowly we became conscious of the fact that the man was clothed in something other than light. He was clad in ochre. At first he had some difficulty in speaking, which inevitably happens to any man after his meditation.

I was so lost in contemplating the radiance that still lingered on his face, that I had not heard him speak. Long after he had begun I noticed his voice saying "Udarata, Vishswa-maitri, tolerance and world-amity are the two truths struggling into life out of the decay of the past. The past is dead. In Benares now you find no youth. Only middle-aged and old people everywhere. But go near Gandhi, you will find youth, nothing but youth. It is all dead here. Gandhi has killed our formalistic life by bringing more life into India."

"Sounds like a paradox," murmured my American fellow-traveler.

"However, it is true," went on the master. "There are two ways of killing: one by dealing death, and the other by giving it life. No formal religion can live if a few fierce saints are born in it all at once. Formal Hinduism has had too many of them since Rama Krishna, and Vivekananda. The result is before us: too much life has killed most of our rituals. It is a pity other creeds have not had such a good fortune happen to them."

"You seem to rejoice, my lord," I remarked.

"He who does not rejoice at the pain of receiving more life is a dead man."

Now I put forth this idea: "But with the old India her very soul may be given a burial. They are killing caste, seclusion of woman, and distinction of races. In the place of cultured castes you will have a culture-less democracy. You will have India without a soul."

"Not culture," proclaimed Kalirishi; "it is life that I study."

Those words reminded us of our friend, the nail-sitter, who never reads books. The holy man explained himself. "I am very old. I was born during the Revolt of 1857. I heard the tales of barbarity with which the

Hindus acted and also of the atrocities that accompanied their suppression by the British. The end of the revolt put so much fear in our race that it has taken a steady process of healing for seventy years to get nearly half the race beyond cowardice. Only half of the people—the other half is still diseased with fear.

"Gandhiji is the symbol of a fearless generation. Fear has no place in their heart. Youth that is unafraid of the British government cannot be expected to fear caste, seclusion of women, race-line and creed-systems. Just think of this hard orthodox Benares sanctioning the abolition of Pariahood of twenty thousand Pariahs a month ago. Malavyia, the very high priest of bigoted Hinduism, celebrated the occasion here. Hundreds of other outcasts will hear of the miracle wrought by Pandit Malavyia. They in turn will break the ancient traditions and assert their rights. Who began all this? Gandhi, our casteless saint." [1]

"Is it good?" asked Mr. Earl. "So much lawlessness all at once. I saw no end of women join the Gandhi militia in the province of Bombay. I witnessed all the nationalists Hindu and Moslem eat one kind of food, wearing only one kind of uniform. Variety is going from the land. Universal monotony stares India in the face."

Kalirishi held to the course that his mind had already taken. "But you never knew the monotony and bore-

[1] In "Visit India With Me" a more detailed study of this appears.

dom that lay under the old castes, sex-distinction, and race-distinctions. For instance, a man of your culture could not enter a single temple of Benares half a dozen years ago. Why? Because you come from a meat-eating race. If eating vegetables makes a saint, then every sheep is as good as Buddha and Jesus of Nazareth. No, many of our old distinctions were sheepish. They betokened cowardice and death. The new is life, new life."

"Are you too a nationalist?" I asked with some misgiving.

"Shiva, O Shiva," the master swore. "No, I am not a nationalist. I pray for Gandhi and the British both."

"How come?" exclaimed our guest from America, very abruptly I thought.

"It is quite explicable," pleaded the holy man humbly. "Pursuing the spiritual, need not make a man blind to the drift of the subconscious of our fellow-beings. That which is under the conscious of the Hindu people is sound and brave. It is not diseased. We, the monks, are the trustees of that unconscious Self of this land. From the sages of the Upanishads down to the humblest monk of Shankara Math today, it is our duty to watch and to keep pure that Self. For the Self alone can uplift a self. I have given you my diagnosis of the Indian Self. It is no more ill; it is yelling because it is reborn, Aditya varna—sun-clad and vibrant."

"Granted that the Indians are reborn," Mr. Earl

sought further information, "you are taking for granted too much negation of law?"

"The present negation of law is but the reverse side of a 'yes,'" rejoined Kalirishi. "Let me be historical for a moment. From 1870 on I have heard Hindu social reformers, European missionary and other critics 'on social reform.' They thundered against child-marriage, cast oppression, and seclusion of women. Did many families abolish any one of those things amongst the masses? No. Why? None of those critics could point out an alternative course to follow.

"But suddenly comes Gandhi who yokes a 'yea' with the 'nay.' 'Stop marrying early, for you must enlist in the national army. Break down castes that divide, for you want to unite all the Indians. Give up religious bigotry in order to live more spiritual life.' That brave 'yes' instead of the timid social reformer's 'no' caught the ears of the young. And as they gave heed to the yea, the nay was accomplished automatically. In ten years' time Gandhi has given the British another India to deal with."

"Are you for the British leaving India bag and baggage?" I questioned him bluntly. "Or, must they stay on?"

"That is immaterial," he answered readily. "If they go they will remain. And if they remain they will go."

"Another paradox!"

"No paradox, Mr. Earl," soothingly began the holy man. "If the British go Indian bureaucrats, Indian bankers, and Indian soldiers will take their place. These will industrialize India faster than the British. If the latter go, their spirit will permeate India much sooner than if they remained. On the contrary if they stay, in order to endure them and to strive against them, we will have to arm ourselves with greater spiritual powers. Hence it is immaterial whether they stay or go. The same attitude should be maintained by all towards the present revolution. It does not matter whether India wins or England beats India."

"Strange talk this!" I grumbled.

"Not at all strange, my son," Kalirishi spoke with a voice deeply steeped in compassion. "You have a right to take sides, and must fight to crown your side with victory. But at the same time your mind should be so trained that it cannot be cast down by any defeat. You have a right to strive; but you will be a fool to hazard your very soul for victory. Never do that. Beyond good and evil is the urge of your spirit. He who wishes to go beyond must fight for the good with righteous weapons. You have to fight for the good in order to go beyond goodness. So if Gandhi wins it will be just as immaterial as if he were beaten."

"Apathy towards results," mumbled Earl. "Apathy in the Greek sense."

"Be like Benares," exhorted Kalirishi. "Look at this city. About two miles away people are dying like flies of smallpox. Monks of our monastery, doctors and Gandhimen are working for the sick day and night.

Benares is a rich municipality deriving its wealth from the pilgrims. Yet its streets are so dusty that they seem hung with suffocating rags. Just the same its railway station and foreign quarters are kept clean and sanitary. Last night the police beat up Gandhi's soldiers. Today nobody hates the British. This is Benares—always living beyond good and evil. Utterly sterile as regards results, forever fertile as regards striving through the good into the beyond-good. Try to understand this. Not the apathy of a dead man but the equinimity of the Living God is what you should aim to be. No, India is safe, no matter what happens. New life has been put into her. She will survive anything."

"But what about the neglect of rites and rituals? The young people do not give a damn." It was my voice rasping, my ear told me.

"Instead of God-worship, the youth are carried away by India-worship. But if you can save India you will save God," replied the holy man with simplicity.

"That needs some explaining," requested Earl.

"I am explaining too much," laughed the holy man. "It is true that he who explains problems succeeds in explaining them away. However, I shall endeavour to be honest. We, in India, believe that like the trees and animals of a place, its spiritual symbols that men make are local. By looking at a local tiger or a sambur deer we perceive the universalness of life. Similarly by contemplating such symbols of Indian spirituality as Shiva and Parvati, Father and Mother of Creation, we appre-

hend the real meaning of the universe. The quality of
a place is omnipotent. There are tigers in Siberia and
tigers in India; though they are alike yet the quality
of each place has marked its own feline as separate.
We have Jews in Southern India who are different
from the Jews of New Orleans. The mark of India
is indelibly there on the former. Behold the Malabar
Christians of Southern India; they are Indian. You
cannot confuse them with their coreligionists elsewhere. Our Jews, Christians, and our Mohammedans
are as mystically-minded as our Hindus.

"I have heard more than one Arab Mohammedan
denounce his Indian fellow-believers as heterodox and
heathen. I have heard Palestinian Jews disown the practices of our Malabar Jews. No matter what community
you take, if it has lived long enough in India it will
bear the marks of that other-worldliness which has
been the main feature of our spirit for fifty centuries.
As the Isha Upanishad put it at the remote dawn of
history, so it is now: Tena tyaktena vunjitha, only by
renouncing this world can you enjoy the true one;
do not envy the path of others, *e.g.,* do not seek to copy
the way of other lands: ma gridha kasy sviddhanam.

"This land is unique. Every effort should be made
to preserve its uniqueness. You cannot do that without
worshipping it. If you save this matrix of the gods she
will give birth to a new set of gods. The gods—
Brahma, Vishnu, Shiva and others are India's creation.
He who neglects the gods and immolates himself for

his love of this Hindustan is as religious as the man who loses his ego by achieving deep spiritual experience through meditation."

"It is spiritual then, this Gandhi movement," I commented.

"No," dissented the master. "This movement is neither spiritual nor material. Only spiritually minded persons get an experience of life larger than their personalities by joining it. This puts the stamp of the spirit on the movement. If a coward practices non-violence by enduring bludgeoning he gets humiliation and nothing else from it. But a brave-souled one gets out of it spirituality. Every large movement is like a religion. One man finds God through it, while another expresses his talent for priestcraft and gets no further."

"Look here, my lord, I want your guidance in a very important matter," I now begged for his advice. "I feel deeply about this movement for independence. Even if we don't win in fact we have won in the realm of thought. Our minds are freed of cant. Now for complete separation of India from the British Empire—do you think we should think and feel this attitude?"

Kalirishi smiled at me as if I were naive as a babe. "Why can't you say what you feel?"

"You see, it looks so ridiculous, our proclaiming India free may look like Don Quixote's imagining giants in a windmill. You recall how he came to grief after his charge."

The holy one cast a glance that seemed to cut and scorch its way into my very soul. "I see you want to stand for freedom without being ridiculed. No doubt, those enemies of ours are most destructive who seek to kill us with ridicule. Alas, I am afraid, he who makes no enemies has put none of his friends to any proof. A man must make good enemies, for they alone purify him of timid friends. India too must test out her friends."

"In other words, you want freedom for India," Mr. Earl animadverted.

"Mr. Earl," questioned my master, "how is it your country, which is founded on a revolution, frowns upon all revolutions?"

"Oh, that is easy to explain," Earl answered readily. "You see in recent years we have had to witness too many tiresome revolutions. Mexico has been staging uprisings by the dozen at our very door-step, proving the futility of such events. China staged a revolution in 1912 which was engineered by the Chinese educated in America. The chaos wrought in China is appalling. It is still going strong. At last we have no stomach for any more. I think, any Hindu that talks for a revolution and a free India to a group of Americans does not afford a convincing spectacle. You said that he may look like Don Quixote. I assure you that he will look like something much worse. If he stand for complete freedom he will appear as Tartarin in the Alps to American businessmen."

The holy man laughed out aloud. Mr. Earl joined him. There was nothing else for me to do but to follow their example.

As I was taking my leave for the day, the master said to me, "Independence, or Dominion Status, give me your most loyal pledge that you will never hate any British man, woman, or child; and that you will strive for your end with non-violence in thought, word, and deed. You see when your old holy man of "My Brother's Face" was dying he indicated to me something. Now his word has come true. You did me the honour to come to me for guidance in your hour of indecision. But India's freedom is not as important as the salvation of your soul. Work as long as you can without fear and hate. But the moment you feel that violence has begun to cloud your mind, your word, or your conduct, abandon everything, go into solitude, and pray 'til you are free. Free your Self from yourself. It is much easier to free India than to keep yourself free of hate, fear, and vanity. If my words seem weak permit me to quote the greatest warrior of ancient India, Bhishma. The old warrior lying on his deathbed urged Karna, the young hero: 'O Karna, fight moved by thy desire for the higher world, without hate and without vindictiveness. Fight in accordance with thy courage and through righteous acts. If you wish I shall pray God to keep you hateless and fearless. Go forth mailed in righteousness and amity."

LETTER XXI

THINGS THAT MATTER

LETTER XXI

THINGS THAT MATTER

HAVING settled the question of my loyalty to my country, the next day when we called on the holy man at about the same hour, we discussed matters that are more vital than patriotism. It was my friend, John Earl, who set the theme of our discussion.

He asked Kalirishi: "Why do you, who have no patriotism, cherish so deep a reverence for Mahatma Gandhi? After all, you are a much bigger holy man than he."

The master laughed softly. It sounded like the mewing of a catbird. "Mr. Earl," he asked, "do all Americans exercise the art of overpraise as well as yourself?"

"Praising," Earl answered brazenly, "is a component part of the air we breathe. But in your case I spoke the truth."

"My reverence for Gandhi springs from my complete trust in his sincerity and his spiritual powers. His moral purity is no whit less than that of Jesus and Buddha. If you go and live with the man a year you shall be convinced of it. There is only one thing he lacks: namely, mysticism. He does not care for superrational experiences. Yet at the same time he can meditate longer than any mystic. He can fast forty days in the wilderness, resisting all the temptations that the human mind and body are exposed to. No, the man's spiritual stature is almost immeasurable.

"But none of his big qualities compels tribute of me. It is his minor merits that have ravished me. Had you lived as long as I have and seen Indian manhood go through the three phases of mental unbalance, you would grasp me easily. In the seventies of the last century all the Indian intelligentsia went wild over the programme of Christianizing this country. High caste persons like Madusudhan Dutt, Kali Banerji, Keshub's young son, and women like Brahmin Rambai—all were converted to Anglo-Saxon Protestantism. They did not stop there; they urged the rest of the country to accept Protestantism, as the final form of Christ's teachings.

"In the nineties came another craze. This time it was Science. Scientific monism, agnosticism, and social reform were the triple intoxicant that the intelligentsia took. That too failed to reach the masses. Soon the intoxication too wore off.

"With the twentieth century came nationalism. 'India for the Indians,' they cried themselves hoarse. Fortunately for the nation the holy men like Vivekananda, Dyananda, Guru Narayaua, and others paid no heed to the ravings of educated classes. They sought to devise a machinery through which the Indian masses can be kindled into an awareness of their great past in order to preserve its best. By the time the World War had begun, literally hundreds of holy men had been trained and sent out to the villages to tell the peasants this: 'Arise, awake, in you the unique culture of India has taken shelter. Preserve it, fight for it now that the alien ideas are threatening it with death.'

"Suddenly from South Africa came Gandhi who had arrived at the same conclusions as our holy men. After testing it out through the most serious trials of over twenty years, Gandhism was put forth before the masses and the educated classes. The latter ran from it as from a pestilence. The former put their trust in it and began to follow this new holy man. The first test than Gandhism went through was very near here, at Champaran. About a dozen years ago the oppressed peasantry of Champaran district went on a tax-strike. Every educated man abused them for embarking on such foolishness. Despite great hardships and severe discouragements the peasants triumphed. The government had to give in. This was Gandhi's first victory on the Indian soil. It went like an earthquake, shaking the minds of the pro-European Indians. It hurt their conceit terribly.

"From that time on, we, the monks of India, kept an eye on the Mahatma. Year by year his reputation grew. Now it has spread over the world. His biography is well known. That Gandhi has saved India is not a doubtful fact. He has spurned the overwhelming faith that people put in modern industrialism; he has tram-

pled upon the god of wealth, and last of all has proved
to the Indian masses that the greatness of a nation
is to be found in its soul-power and not in sword-force.

"Behold, the masses are awakened. The ancient
verities of the East are on the march. Moses, Jesus,
Mohammed, Zoroaster, Buddha, and Confucius reiterated that stupendous discovery of the Asiatic genius,
that life at its core is spiritual. And that the surest
way to fight violence is through non-violence. The
Europeans owe their religion to Asia. They cannot dis-
pute this truth. We are supreme in the realm of religion. For from time immemorial the Asiatics have
made God and the Soul as the objects of intense
research.

"And the most important statements and the largest
experiments on non-violence were made by the Orientals. Whether it be the Jews persecuted by the Chris-
tions in Europe, or, Armenians persecuted by the
Turks in Asia, it is these two Oriental races along with
innumerable Hindus who have paid the largest price
for non-violent resistance. In the laboratory of soul-
research we, the Asians, are the teachers not learners.
In fact our studies in human spirituality have been
given the most important place in all history.

"May I go further and brag that God, when He
incarnates on earth without any human father, chooses
an Asiatic woman for His mother? It has been so in
the past—so shall it be in the future. Goods-making is
our largest business. Our science, our art, and our

philosophy come after. Gandhi is nothing new. He is
the reincarnation of our ancient Asian psyche. He has
taught our masses not to be afraid of poverty as the
northern races of Europe seem to be. He has taught
them that though they are disarmed, they can act as
heroes. Instead of considering our weaponlessness a
source of cowardice, it should be and now it has been
converted into an overwhelming sign of courage. Non-
violent resistance is more heroic an act than the organized scientific violence of an army.

"To be ill-clad in this tropical climate is not immoral,
but natural; poverty is not a handicap but a leaping
board to venturesome experiences of living. India's
other-worldliness, last of all, which he has revealed to
our people, has a great deal to teach the European
world. Though in the realm of science we must sit at
the feet of the West another half century, yet in the
science of soul-culture we are the teachers of the West
as Asia always has been.

"Now you know why I admire our toothless, rab-
bit-eared Gandhi. He has saved our masses from the
worst aspect of north European culture. It is a pity
that we have never been exposed to its best. Industrialism, wealth-worship, militarism, and middle class
humanitarianism are not the very best products of the
European genius. We should not mistake them for
their betters. Now the educated Indians are being purified: they have learned that they did not always succeed
in discovering and assimilating the topmost reach of

the European spirit. Their misunderstanding has harmed Europe just as much as it has hurt us. Instead of being a bridge between the most excellent qualities of the two, they fell into the pit of the second rate. No, all India owes Gandhi a great debt of gratitude. Even if he died tomorrow the spiritual force that he has let loose upon the country will go on working in our character. . . . My son, I have talked enough. Let me stop."

Seeing that the chance for asking my most momentous question was almost gone, I begged Kalirishi earnestly: "Please enlighten me, do you personally want the British to go?"

He smiled compassionately at my remark. "Why send them away empty? They came here for gold. In spite of taking what they could they still feel poor. For money cannot enrich any race. We have not yet given them God who alone enriches people permanently."

"God!" exclaimed Earl as if he were in a daze.

"Why God!" I wished to know the master's mind more deeply.

He laughed at both of us: "Are you startled by the word God? It seems, you never hear it very often. Let me assure you, if you saw Him, He wouldn't bite." Kalirishi shut his eyes, and entered into meditation. Earl and I eyed each other fearing that the morning's interview had come to an end: the holy one had probably gone back into his silence.

Just that instant he opened his eyes. His gaze was full of joy. "No, I was not running away from you," he remarked. "One's guests are God. That is what the old books say. I for myself like to see the British taught various techniques of God-realization, before their final departure hence. Our monasteries have saved up real techniques that will enrich the European soul if it could acquire them. There is an impression abroad that finding God is a matter of shutting one's eyes. But that is not the truth. For instance, we have well wrought techniques of meditating with our eyes and mind open. Sitting thus, gazing in this manner . . . you see."

"How many techniques have we?" I requested for more information. .

"We have as many as there are human beings. Not one religion for all, but each soul must make a perfect technique that will give it God." The holy one's words had a touch of finality. "For instance, Bhakti Yoga, the art of finding Him through Love, has over seven techniques. One may develop his relation to God as a son to his Father, another as a father to his Son, still another as a sister with her Brother. Each one of the methods is pragmatically sound. Alas, the deeper aspect of what I am saying cannot be printed. . . . There are people in India now who have found Him through the constant practice of one relationship or another. Finding the Lord is no talk. It is a science. Our country has an elaborate science of spirituality.

It should be given to the world through the British. No use sending them away without it. Let us train them in our spiritual arts before they leave."

"How did you find God, through what technique?" our American guest inquired.

At this question the master shut his eyes once more. A long pause followed. The stillness about us grew more and more intense every minute. Outside noises, such as, the pilgrims' chant, the vendors' cries, and temple bells became quieter; and at last stilled. Many minutes must have passed ere Kalirishi spoke again. "My technique!" He uttered his words in such a low tone that we had to strain our hearing to the utmost in order to understand. "My temperament is not that of a God-lover. I am a God-knower. I studied science in the University. Took my degree in physics. Then just when my parents pressed me to marry and settle down I renounced my professorship and went to the Shankara Monastery at Nasik. There I met one of the apostles of Rama Krishna. This man was His chela.

"After examining my temperament for months he initiated me into Jnana. He taught me my technique of knowing God. After persistent practices of six or seven hours a day for fifteen years I got a glimpse. . . . Let me use the words of our elder seers; for they alone adequately describe Him. As the fire leaps out of many logs of many shapes so He sprang from every being that I beheld. As the wind blows drawing deep and steep music from forests and mountain crests so

He draws from each soul the terrible tones of His
Presence. As the eye of the world, the sun, shines on
filth and sandalwood, yet is not tainted nor rendered
fragrant; so He the dweller in each person is not col-
ored by their good or evil deeds. Seated as One in
all, He hammers out of Himself those flames and
sparks that men call the Many. He alone gives peace.
He alone exists. Seeing Him rooted in your heart you
leap over the chasm of unrest. He alone frees you of
the snare of Good and Evil. The Eternal in all the
eternals, the Consciousness behind all that is conscious,
the dancer, One, in the garbs of Many, the nullifier
and fulfiller I have found Him, I have found Him.
. . . Hearken unto me, O sons of immortality! He is
the supremest light. Even the fiercely shining sun
seems but a mask drawn over His Face. Hearken, and
gaze with me into His eyes. . . .

"You know, you young men are most seductive.
You have made me tell of things that I never mention. What was your question that made me digress? I
am afraid I have lost it. Hand me the thread, my son."

"I too had forgotten all about it. Perhaps this question will do as well: What was God's purpose in tying
up India with the British these many years?"

"Why should God have any purpose?" the holy one
answered without the slightest pondering. "But we can
invent a purpose of our own. The British have given
us a world-language through which India's wisdom
must be given to all mankind. As the Roman Empire

and Latin served the cause of Pauline Christianity, so shall the British Empire and Shakespeare's mother tongue be a medium through which our Indian spirituality will travel to all the races on earth. Indian poet-scholars must translate our thoughts into the most poetic and accurate English. Indian holy men must travel everywhere and teach our techniques of finding God. And those of you who go to America and England to learn modern science must take with you some product of our culture to impart to those whom you meet. Do not go out empty-handed. Go panoplied with God. If you carry Him, the Highest, on your back with the stubbornness of a mule you will be able to receive in exchange the highest that they have to give. It will save you from accepting their second rate creations."

It was getting late by now. Before taking our leave Earl asked Kalirishi: "How can you establish that the human soul fell from perfection, and it is struggling to return to that state?"

"That, Mr. Earl," the master said in answer, "needs no establishing. Our homesickness for perfection is so great that it drives us on searching for Him. Even if it could be proved that we never went astray from the Heart of God, that would bring us no peace. Peace we can win only when we are conscious that we are in that Heart whose never-ending light lighteth all— Tasya vasa sarvam idam bibhati. It does not matter whether we fell or not. What matters is our acquiring

that continuous awareness of Him now. Any 'continuous' awareness will do that for you. If you can be
conscious of that wall yonder uninterruptedly, through
and beyond all time, it will give you bliss. But the
trouble is that in case the wall collapsed you would
be interrupted. That which can be stopped at any
moment is imperfect. The trouble with an objective
awareness is that it comes to an end. But suppose you
have a constant awareness—that you are life, death,
and beyond, then you will have bliss. Falling away,
and returning to God, are utterly immaterial ideas
if those hypotheses fail to strike fire and cannot illumi-
nate you to a state of perpetual consciousness. Train
yourself. . . . Do not waste time on many hypotheses.
Your way of meditation that you described to me
recently is a good technique. . . . Follow it, as you have
more than a quarter of a century. After all, it is not a
very long meditation. Return to me after five years
more. If I am alive; probably we shall see Him
together. Yes, I guarantee the Vision. Mind, you keep
on doing every day what you and I have discussed.
Yes, Mr. Earl, the bond between you and me is a
long-standing one. Even if I die I shall have to serve
you. Now, farewell. Do not talk prematurely. No,
do not write letters. I never read them. You will be
brought here to me by Him when you are ready.
Farewell." The master lifted his hand and gave my
friend a special blessing. "Amritasya navayi—may you
realize that you are the very artery of Immortality."

That afternoon we left Benares. From the curve of the road we took a last look at the holy city. It rose sheer from the diamond-colored river, tier upon tier, in serried ranks of flagstones and towers. It seemed to say, "I am the many-branched tree of Truth, the summit of sanctities, the gold behind the dross of things, the secret hidden behind the sun. Behold me, the chalice of Immortality."

The pilgrims who were going out with us saluted Kashi for the last time, chanting: "Truth-clad city."

CONCLUSION!

THE most important issue in India's struggle today is the effect that will be produced on her ancient culture. This culture is still a vital force in the masses of her people expressing itself continuously in each act and word of every-day life.

The Western idea of democratic self-government has fired the popular imagination and will find expression. It came to us largely through the World War, the war of the Western Powers, which has caused a ferment in so many countries.

The war was fought to make the world safe for democracy! The peace treaty was drawn up on the principle of self-determination of nations. India was asked to send troops to the war and she understood that Dominion Status was promised. She sent the troops and feels that she has been betrayed by the war. The result appears to be an irrepressible conflict if Dominion Status is not granted.

All the histories agree that the English went to India for a business purpose, to make money. The East India Company was a purely mercantile company. The victories of Clive and Warren Hastings were the natural development of the venture. Young India believes that she remains there because of her financial interests.

Rudyard Kipling, on the other hand, places England in India to carry on the White Man's burden. If the principles enunciated in connection with the late war are sound, democracy and the self-determination of nations, a few English have no right to govern the great country of India with millions of inhabitants in opposition to the will of that people. The matter should be left to a plebiscite. However, as my main interest is the spiritual and cultural future of India, I shall leave these questions as to the proper basis of government for the historians to discuss.

It will not do to end this book without telling the reader why I want India to win her independence through non-violent resistance.

Ever since the war I have been driven to the conclusion that without moral means no noble end can be achieved. It took that colossal display of violence to convince many men that the world can not be set free by forces that are not completely spiritual. The culture of India cannot continue if the action which she takes to express herself, to preserve her ancient traditions, arts, and industries, is not in harmony with that culture.

It is not only a revolution or violence that we have to fear in the present crisis but concomitant civil war. Revolutions of violence commonly lead to civil war sooner or later, as the nation is torn from its traditions and different classes of the community come in conflict with each other. But it is my firm belief that if a revolution can be accomplished through non-violence it will bring no disastrous effects with it. Spiritual enthusiasm will destroy the jealousies that have existed between Indian classes and creeds. The severe discipline that non-violence imposes on the thoughts and actions of its votaries, be they Hindus or Moslems, will purify them of religious bigotry. As a well-drilled pearl obeys the thread that unites it with other pearls of a garland, so the penance of non-violence will unite the people of India with an unbreakable spirit of unity.

In reaching this conclusion, I have perhaps been unduly influenced by actually seeing the Gandhi movement in operation. By applying the methods of the Christian and other holy books to a political struggle petty animosities between those engaged in it have disappeared. The whole world recognizes the significance of Christ's words to Peter, when he smote the servant of the High Priest and cut off his right ear, "Put up thy sword"! It was a great gain to the cause of Christianity that Christ refused to fight for religious truth. He unflinchingly asserted it but, if there was to be violence on that account, it must be the violence of others. Gandhi asserts young India's belief in the political truth that all men are entitled to life, liberty and the pursuit of happiness and "that to secure these rights governments are instituted among men deriving their just powers from the consent of the governed." His followers assert this truth, but if there is violence on that account it will not be theirs.

In the World War I felt that there was much hate. Terrible stories of atrocities by enemies had to be told to whet animosity. Among those who practice non-resistance, on the other hand, the prevailing feeling is one of profound pity that the affairs of the world are so tangled that the English, holding India only by force of arms, feel compelled to strike those who are asserting their natural rights. As to the other party to the conflict, the spiritual grandeur of non-violent revolution must have its effect on even the most extreme British militarist.

But one word more! This non-violent revolution, if it succeeds, may prove an epoch-making event in world history. Not only does passive resistance create a purer spiritual atmosphere, it will actually prevent most of the death, wounding and destruction which war involves. The limit is soon reached, where soldiers will refuse to strike or kill the defenseless. India has given many religions to the world. She may now be giving a new method of gaining political freedom without resort to war.

AS A PRINCE SEES IT

THOUGH during my recent stay in India I had no chance to interview a Maharajah I think the American reader should be acquainted with what a representative Hindu ruler thinks of the present unrest.

The full text of the Maharajah of Bikanir's * statement of July 18 to the Associated Press of India on the subject of the correspondence exchanged between the Viceroy, on the one hand, and Sir Tej Bahadur Sapru and Mr. Jayakar on the other, has reached this country. [A brief summary of the statement from Reuter's correspondent at Simla appeared in *The Times* on July 21.] The Maharajah's statement opened with a reference to the political situation, which "cannot but cause the gravest anxiety to the Princes and States who, through treaties of alliance and friendship, are bound by indissoluble ties to the Crown . . . by friendship and attachment to the British Empire, and by the most patriotic feelings to their own country."

After expressing the fullest confidence in Lord Irwin, concurring with the views expressed by Sir Tej Bahadur Sapru and Mr. Jayakar in their letter to the Viceroy, and describing any rejection of the hand of friendship proffered by the British Government as a grave blunder, the Maharajah said:

"It is obviously impossible for the British Government to approach the Congress leaders for a cessation of the non-cooperation movement. I have now taken active part in the administration of my State for 32 years and am a firm believer in strong rule. Any challenge to the supremacy of a Government—whether it be the British Government or the Government of an Indian State—must inevitably be taken up. Revolution, or forces moving towards revolution, must be put down; and no Government worthy of the name can abdicate its functions. But it of course follows that side by side with firmness the rule must be beneficent, just, and sympathetic, and at the same time tempered with mercy; and it is

---

* The Maharajah of Bikanir signed the Versailles Treaty for India. This year he is leading the Indian delegates to the League of Nations.

no less essential that we should not be handicapped by any false notions or mistaken considerations of prestige. . . . It therefore follows that wise statesmanship and the interests of India as well as of the Empire demand that every avenue possible should be explored and every opportunity wisely, tactfully, and sympathetically taken advantage of to bring about more cordial and closer relations between the Government and the people. As I pointed out at Guildhall 13 years ago, people who hold that India can be ruled at the point of the sword do a grave injustice to both Great Britain and India, and that the retention of the British connexion—in which I, in common with my brother Princes, am a firm believer—must rest on much firmer foundations than force. . . .

"Again, in 1917, I ventured to bring home the fact that India even then was changing very rapidly and beyond the conception of those who —on the strength of former residence or service in India, or, while residing in England all the time, have had official connexion with this country—pose as critics of those who have had the burden and responsibility and the duty of carrying on the King-Emperor's Government out here. It is impossible for them really to be aware of the remarkable changes going on, or appreciate the situation as it now exists in India.

"I own a house and spend a month or two every year at the seaside, in Bombay—admittedly the present storm-centre in India—and, though I was ill for part of the time, yet throughout my stay there last May and June I kept my eyes and ears open, and was able to go about and see things for myself, and I also met frequently several loyal moderate and liberal friends among British Indian leaders. I can thus claim to speak with some authority . . . when I testify to the extremely grave situation and the unmistakable depth and force of the widespread national awakening. The movement has taken a firm hold on people of practically all classes and communities of Indians, at least in the Bombay Presidency, including a very large percentage of the commercial community. . . . No doubt with all the power and resources at the command of Great Britain, a great Government like the British Government, with a mighty Empire at its back, can ultimately crush . . . this movement. But even then the struggle is not likely to end as quickly as some may imagine and the situation . . . is apt to get worse before it gets better. . . . In the meanwhile there will be created in an ever-increasing degree intense and widespread feelings of bitterness and hatred—the incalculable harm arising from which it is impossible fully to foresee at the present moment."